FOREWORD BY
BRIAN MCLAREN

THE HIDDEN POWER OF
ELECTRONIC CULTURE

HOW MEDIA SHAPES FAITH,
THE GOSPEL, AND CHURCH

Z ZONDERVAN®

ZONDERVAN.com/
AUTHOR**TRACKER**
follow your favorite authors

We want to hear from you. Please send your comments about this book to us in care of zreview@zondervan.com. Thank you.

ZONDERVAN®

The Hidden Power of Electronic Culture: How Media Shapes Faith, the Gospel, and Church
Copyright 2005 by Shane A. Hipps.

Youth Specialties resources, 300 S. Pierce St., El Cajon, CA 92020 are published by Zondervan, 5300 Patterson Ave. SE, Grand Rapids, MI 49530.

Library of Congress Cataloging-in-Publication Data

Hipps, Shane A.
  The hidden power of electronic culture : how media shapes faith, the Gospel, and church / Shane A. Hipps.
    p. cm.
  Includes bibliographical references.
  ISBN 978-0-310-26274-9 (pbk.)
  1. Christianity and culture. 2. Mass media—Influence. 3. Mass media—Religious aspects—Christianity. 4. Technology—Religious aspects—Christianity. 5. Popular culture—Religious aspects —Christianity.   I. Title.
BR115.C8H56 2005
261.5'2—dc22

                                                                      2005024206

Web site addresses listed in this book were current at the time of publication. Please contact Youth Specialties via e-mail (YS@YouthSpecialties.com) to report URLs that are no longer operational and replacement URLs if available.

Interior design by Mark Novelli

Printed in the United States of America

08 09 10 11 12 13 • 20 19 18 17 16 15 14 13 12 11 10 9 8 7 6 5 4

FOR ANDREA
MY BRIDE, MY HEARTBEAT, MY HOME

TABLE OF CONTENTS

GRATITUDES

Writing has never been an easy process for me. It's like birthing an elephant. While I'll never know how that actually feels, this image repeatedly visited me during the writing of this book. It was a pregnancy that lasted over a year. It was not without joy or anticipation, but the labor pains were often unyielding and the outcome was perpetually uncertain. Fortunately, I was not alone. All along the way I had midwives to facilitate the birth. I am deeply grateful for their support, participation, and guidance.

First and foremost, my deepest gratitude is reserved for Andrea, my wife. Not only was she a profoundly supportive spouse who absorbed the tremendous ups and downs of the writing journey, but she also served as a most faithful reader. Andrea refused to accept the ideas that wandered into dense philosophical abstraction. Instead she helped me find a voice that emanated from my heart rather than my head alone. If this book connects with you at all, I owe those places to her.

Without the guidance and encouragement of Tony Jones, this book would have never happened. He was the one who first prodded me to turn my ideas into a book, something I had never remotely considered. But more than this, he personally sponsored my proposal before the emergentYS editorial board and argued that it was a book worth printing. Needless to say, he must have been persuasive.

I owe much of the content in Part I of this book to Read Mercer Schuchardt. He first introduced me to Marshall McLuhan's writings and personally guided me through the deep and murky waters of the little-known field of media ecology—the theoretical perspective that informs this entire book.

Mark Lau Branson, Jim Brenneman, and Pasadena Mennonite Church are the primary sources for the ideas found in Part II of this book. As a professor, Mark gave me the language and resources for thinking about the church. As my pastor, Jim gave me a platform to participate in shaping the church. As my community, the people of Pasadena Mennonite Church showed me how to live as the church.

I would also like to thank Tim Hartman, Danielle Hample, Ross Mueller,

Ryan White, Bob and Amy Anderson, Chad Becker, Mike Rewers, Jim Gribnitz, Ben Davis, Andy Bennett, Emrys Tyler, and Brad Lounsberry. These friends generously served as faithful readers, offering me invaluable, honest, and open feedback on the manuscript. It is an infinitely better book because of them.

Finally, I would like to thank my brother Brad Hipps, a gifted writer who made my prose and logic more lucid, and my parents, Jack and Sheila Hipps, who planted and nurtured an intellectual curiosity in me from a very young age. In addition, they read the manuscript with great care and thoughtfulness and offered unrelenting enthusiasm and encouragement during the writing process.

You have all been abiding blessings to me. Thank you.

FOREWORD

I have mixed feelings about the term "emerging church." Yes, I believe some new and exciting things are emerging. But I think they're emerging not in one movement or among one group of people and certainly not along one model, but rather in diverse ways across the spectrum of the church—in spaces ranging from cathedrals to storefronts, from country chapels to urban pubs and living rooms.

These emerging realities aren't the brainchildren of any single leader or organization: They're springing up spontaneously, literally around the world. People are finding one another and saying, "What? You too? I thought I was the only one."

What's going on? What's behind or beneath these changes? Are there common subterranean sources nourishing these global shifts?

Critics say it's all surface, style, and cosmetics—nothing substantial, just pandering to and accommodating the latest fads and consumer demands. Others chalk it up to "new methods" for the "unchanging message." Participants themselves are often moving to new practices, thinking, and values somewhat intuitively—they can't explain what's going on any better than anybody else.

That's where Shane Hipps comes in. Aided by the work of one of the most important creative thinkers of the 20th century, Marshall McLuhan, Shane excavates beneath the surface layers to some deep insights that I'll bet you've never considered before. I know he has helped me see new dimensions to the dangers and opportunities hidden both in the status quo and in the new emerging realities of the church.

Have you ever considered the powerful impact of the printing press? Can you imagine the pre-printing-press church—a church without Bibles, without hymnals, without bulletins (impossible!)? But Shane takes us deeper, asking how the form of that revolutionary 16th-century technology has affected the church—its piety, its authority structures, its structures of theology, its forms of public worship, its very articulation of the gospel.

Then consider the impact of electronic media—telegraph, radio, film, television, computer, the Internet, even the projection screen. How did and how will these innovations rewire our minds and change the way churches function—in piety, in authority structures, in structures of theology, in forms of public worship, in the articulation of the gospel?

I thought about this a good deal even before reading Shane's work, partly because I read McLuhan back in the 1970s. But Shane sharpened a number of issues for me and left me sometimes murmuring, "So that's why..." and other times worrying, "Oh, no...I hadn't thought about that."

Before your church launches into another round of "worship wars" (whether your battle lines are on the contemporary or emerging church front), read this book. You still might have some arguments, but they'll be better ones, deeper ones. You'll be paying attention to the bulk of the iceberg you've never seen from the surface. The outcomes will be more worthwhile and lasting.

Reading McLuhan years ago for me was, as it is for many people, tough and sometimes maddening—slow going through convoluted thinking but yielding flashes of insight that made the hard slogging well worth it. Shane's prose by contrast is lucid, clear, and enjoyable, and it's hard to believe, but the same quality of insights come through without the literary pain. It's not exactly "McLuhan for Dummies," but it's an intelligent yet intelligible appropriation of McLuhan for today's Christian leaders.

For those testing the waters, trying to decide whether it's worthwhile to make a break with the standard traditional or contemporary church, this book will serve as an excellent primer, focusing less on esoteric intellectual history and more on right-in-your-own-living-room social history (especially the sociology and psychology of the media).

For those already knee-deep in the emerging church conversation, this book will help us avoid unwise overreactions as it warns us from being used by the tools we think we're using. It will also help sensitize us to the ways our methods can contradict our message—and with a message as important as ours, that's a needed sensitivity! Everyone who reads these pages will come away with a renewed sense of the importance of the local church and the quest for authentic community in particular, a quest that is at once helped and hampered by cell phones, e-mail, websites, blogs, and the rest of our digital universe.

A Christian publisher recently told me there is some concern in his field about the passing of a generation of respected authors (I won't mention names); the dependable mainstays of the publishing world are aging, retiring, and passing away, and many wonder who will replace them. While reading Shane's book, I felt deeply encouraged by the quality of his work—as well as the work of many fine young writers making their debuts these days. These are thoughtful people, well educated (in the best sense of the word), and skilled writers, and they speak well for the future of the church in these challenging times. emergentYS is to be congratulated for finding emerging talents like Shane and making sure their messages are made accessible to the rest of us.

Yes, it's in the form of a book, and yes, mass-produced books are part of modernity's legacy. But as Shane wisely points out, we'd be foolish to lose the skills we've gained during the print era. Balanced minds cannot live on websites and chat rooms alone. It's important to remember that every innovation is an amputation as well as an extension—and if you don't know what that means, then read and digest this book you're now holding.

— **Brian McLaren**, pastor (crcc.org), author (anewkindofchristian.com)

INTRODUCTION

My professional life began in the corporate world—in advertising to be specific. It is an industry reminiscent of college fraternities, comprised mostly of creative young people who prefer to stay young and can't stand the thought of wearing suits to work. In many ways it's the youth ministry of the corporate world, except the trips to exotic locations are for TV shoots instead of mission trips, and advertisers are accountable to clients rather than parents.

I worked as an account manager and later as a strategic planner on a variety of brands. I spent time working on everything from the Minnesota Anti-Smoking campaign to Harrah's Entertainment, Inc. (i.e., casinos). However, the majority of my career was spent working on Porsche Cars North America with a team that developed, managed, and executed nearly all aspects of a multimillion-dollar communications plan.

Overall, my job and much of my training were devoted to studying media's effect on consumer habits. It was work that required me to have a firm understanding of media theory and to keep a finger on the pulse of cultural change. I became what people in the industry call a "consumer anthropologist," an elaborate term that simply describes a person whose task is understanding various consumer subcultures, what they influence, and what influences them.

I was having a great time, but throughout my career I was aware of a nascent feeling that I wasn't doing the thing I was made for. I ignored the feeling as often as possible. After all, I enjoyed what I was doing, was well compensated, and felt I was using my talents. But as I began to study the writings of communications theorist Marshall McLuhan, it became nearly impossible to keep that nagging feeling under the surface. He opened my eyes to the profoundly negative ways advertising shapes our culture, an impact I could see in the church as well.

Ironically, my study of McLuhan was something I embarked upon in order to deepen a particular skill set for my career. It wasn't until I read Dietrich Bonhoeffer's *The Cost of Discipleship* that I realized I could no longer continue in that career; I was spending 70 hours a week devoted to something that was antithetical to my most deeply held beliefs. The most effective, award-winning, and respected advertising is that which convinces consumers that a product or service will meet their spiritual and emotional needs. In this sense, the measure of my success in advertising was my ability to promote a counterfeit gospel.

With the encouragement of my courageous wife and input from our church community, I left advertising to attend seminary and pursue my long-held interest in theology. During my time at seminary I began to see the myriad ways in which my previous training and knowledge could translate to better understanding the challenges facing the church. It was the confluence of these two areas of interest and expertise that led to the ideas found in this book.

This is not a book intended to argue that the church needs to engage culture. Rather, it assumes cultural engagement is well underway. It presupposes that there are changes already happening in churches and that people are wrestling with difficult questions about the true message of the gospel, the balance between cultural relevancy and faithfulness to the gospel, and what it means to be the church in our electronic consumer culture. This book seeks to explore these issues and provide some insight into the often unintended consequences—both good and bad—of how we go about living as the church.

The following chapters are aimed at people who are trying new things or trying to make old things work in new ways; when forced to choose, I much prefer to hold back the stallion of aggressive change than to kick the mule of stolid church tradition. There are vast libraries of books that have done a thorough job of "kicking the mule," and to contribute another boot to its hindquarters would be redundant at best.

ANTICIPATING UNINTENDED CONSEQUENCES

For several summers during college I worked as a counselor for a youth adventure camp in Michigan. One part of my job was to lead hiking and canoe trips in various parts of North America. Weeks prior to the campers' arrival we counselors were led through a series of training exercises by seasoned outdoorsmen to prepare us for the rigors of these trips.

Like all good training sessions, this time involved an assortment of team-building exercises. One in particular stands out for me: We were to raise the camp flag. The problem was there was no flagpole, and we were given only one hour to find a solution. They provided us with some basic cutting tools, a rope, and a metal O-ring for hoisting the flag, and that was it.

Immediately, our team went into action. Some of us charged into the woods with saws and axes in search of a suitable pole. Others began digging a hole deep in the ground where the pole would be set. The deadline was closing in when our peers emerged triumphantly from the wilderness with a freshly cut and stripped tree trunk ready for placement. Upon placing our new pole, we quickly began filling the hole with dirt. Then we implemented our most innovative idea: We stabilized the pole by wedging large stones down around its base, ensuring the pole would not wobble, sway, or ever come out. With minutes to spare the pole was secure and reaching proudly into the air nearly two stories high. All we had to do was hoist the flag.

At that moment we experienced the phenomenon of near-simultaneous epiphany. It occurred to us that we should have affixed the metal O-ring and the rope to the pole before we erected it. The head scratching didn't last long; we quickly commissioned our best climber to scale the pole with rope and ring in hand. To his surprise, he could get only halfway up the pole. Just barely hanging on, and with no other options, he affixed the O-ring to the midpoint of the pole. After he had arrived safely on the ground, we triumphantly raised the flag.

It was over. We finished on time and began throwing the customary high fives and offering noises of approval, all the while doing our best to ignore the embarrassment of our flag luffing at permanent half-mast.

The flag-raising debacle reflects my experience in the church. More than once in my church life I have enthusiastically set out to help create a new ministry, only to discover we hadn't anticipated the consequences, leaving us with a program flailing at half-mast. I am not alone in this; many people have set out to create a new worship service (or church) designed to attract non-Christians, only to discover that it attracts the opposite—well-versed Christians from other churches in search of new experiences to consume. Whether our big ideas create new problems or simply fail to accomplish our objectives, we often have difficulty anticipating the consequences of our creations.

As we learn to endure what feels like a perpetual metamorphosis in culture, the tasks of ministry are growing increasingly difficult. The changing pressures and complexities of forming God's people take a toll, and the experience we gain from one moment feels irrelevant for the next. Even mundane tasks take on new dimensions we never considered, like creating stable small group structures in a profoundly mobile and commuter culture or teaching a Bible study when our attentions rarely span beyond 10 minutes. Commenting on this reality, theologian Eddie Gibbs once observed that if you have 20 years of ministry experience, it's really more like having one year of experience 20 times.[1]

These challenges can be overwhelming, yet we charge ahead, unaware of the problems we may be creating for ourselves. This book is an invitation to pause before we put the flagpole into the ground and to ask important questions about unintended consequences. In doing so, we will better anticipate possible outcomes and bring new freedom to the challenges and mystery of ministry in our age.

THE NEXT GREAT AWAKENING

For decades our cultural landscape has grown increasingly unfamiliar to the church. We are living through tumultuous chaos and spiritual upheaval typically called postmodernity. The changes in philosophy and culture have altered the place of the church in society. Depending on one's perspective, this shift and its attendant impact on the church is dangerous, irrelevant, wonderful, or just plain terrifying.

In response to changes in our cultural climate, a burgeoning number of churches are experimenting with new forms of worship, new ideas about leadership and community, and a new understanding of the message of the gospel. These churches are commonly known as "emerging" churches. Responding to both the megachurch model of market-driven growth and to the mainline liberal model of church as a "place where the sacraments happen,"[2] emerging churches and their leaders have sought to become dynamic and organic people on a mission. While these churches tend to be rooted in the evangelical tradition, the participants are no longer bound by it. Moving beyond old debates of liberal versus conservative, they are loosening theology from the constraints of evangelical tradition and striving toward a more holistic understanding of what it means to live as Christians in the world. In the process, they are casting off old assumptions about media and technology and engaging culture on its own terms. In many ways this inclination to recast the place and purpose of the church marks the dawn of what I believe will be another great awakening.

THE "WHY?" QUESTIONS

Fueled by changes in our culture, descriptions of and prescriptions for responding to the chaos are being churned out at blender speed. A host of books and articles have been written on *what* has changed in our culture and *how* the church ought to respond to these changes. However, few writers have made a serious effort to understand *why* these changes have occurred. Why are we seeing such drastic changes in our philosophy and cultural topography? Why is postmodernity gaining a foothold in the church? Why do many Christians increasingly see conversion to the Christian faith as a process rather than an event? Why are congregations showing a preference for nonlinear experiences and mystery over propositions and reason?

Answering these questions means going beyond simply describing the changes. When an earthquake hits—and for many the changes in our culture are indeed an ideological earthquake—we must try to understand what caused it and dig deeper to see if there is a way to predict the next tremor and perhaps ride it out with less upheaval.

The answers to these *why* questions are immensely complex. This volume is not intended as an exhaustive understanding of the answers. Instead, it identifies and traces one contour of the mystery. I propose that the answer to the question of why these changes have come about can be found in part by exploring the nature and effects of media and technology on culture.

A CATALYST FOR CONVERSATION AND CREATIVITY

If you have attended conferences or done any reading on the topic of postmodernity and faith, you will find that those empathetic to the postmodern ethos are wary of offering universal solutions for highly contextual dilemmas. I am no exception to this phenomenon—thus I am reluctant to offer hard and fast solutions or answers. This book is more concerned with identifying broader issues that impact the ways we live as the body of Christ. At the same time, it is by no means a simple exercise in abstract thinking. I believe such an exploration would be in vain if it did not yield some pragmatic suggestions for navigating our current cultural context. With this in mind I will make periodic recommendations, some by asking what I believe to be the right questions, others by offering specific examples. All of these should be held with an open hand and assessed in the cultural and theological context of your congregation.

I also want to make it clear that I am not a wholly uncritical advocate of the ways in which the church is responding to cultural change. There are as many challenges for churches who forge ahead blindly as there are for churches who hold on to the old ways out of fear. My desire here is to exhort all of us to slow down and ask different questions as we move forward with discerning minds, authentic hearts, and faithful feet.

This is not simply a book about "how to use media." Rather, it seeks to provide the tools to help us interpret our electronic culture and understand the implications for our faith and our corporate life together. Behind everything that follows is a conviction that within the *forms* of media and technology, regardless of their *content*, are extremely powerful forces that cause changes in our faith, theology, culture, and ultimately the church.

Whether we have been suspicious of or enthusiastic about the cultural changes and innovations in the church, we have developed a shortsighted, two-dimensional view of how electronic culture and media are shaping both the church and the message of the gospel. By listening in on the conversations of a long-forgotten prophet like Marshall McLuhan and revitalizing his wisdom for our times, we restore our ability to perceive both distance and depth amid the wonder and mayhem of our electronic, postmodern culture.

PART I: NEW WAYS TO PERCEIVE

SEEING BUT NOT PERCEIVING

CHAPTER ONE

A few years after I graduated from college, I became a lay leader at my local church. The pastor invited me to join a "task force" (a sexy name for a committee) that was assembled in order to rethink and revamp our contemporary worship service. At the time we had two services: a traditional service featuring an organist and a full choir leading hymns, and a contemporary service featuring a band leading praise music. Our contemporary service was floundering; the attendance was low and the energy lacking.

Our discussions as a task force centered on things like the style of worship leading, an inadequate sound system, and poor acoustics. Eventually, these conversations led us to consider the controversial measure of introducing a projection screen. The vast majority of our debate on this issue concerned questions of costs, logistics, and aesthetics. We wondered where the money would come from. Would the screen be obtrusive? Where would we put it? How would the older generation feel about it? These were all valid and important questions, but we began to believe these were not the most important questions for us to ask.

Our original reason for considering a projection screen was largely imitative—all good contemporary services have one. But as we worked through the issue, we realized the rationale of "everybody is doing it" was flawed, and we began exploring different questions: Why do all contemporary services have a screen? What is the effect of using a projection screen versus using a hymnal or bulletin? How would this new form of media alter the congregation's experience in worship?

After some discussion, we came to the conclusion that a screen frees the body from the bulletin or book. It invites movement, dance, and physical expression in worship. It lifts the heads of congregants, amplifying the sound and energy of their voices. We believed all of these were the chief marks of a "good" contemporary service, and they became our guides as we worked to implement this simple change. While this decision was about a relatively minor concern in the life of our church, there was great value in asking this new set of questions. When we considered the broader implications of a seemingly simple decision, it changed the nature of the debate, freed us from our opposing camps, and opened us to better ways of thinking about the rest of the service.

Our conversation was in no way unique to that church. Nor did our insights reflect a grand breakthrough in understanding worship technology. But I believe we hit on the fundamental issue of the ways in which media affect the gathered community. Unfortunately, these issues are often only raised—if they are raised at all—when dealing with simple forms such as the projection screen. We seem less interested in asking this question about the more pervasive and complex cultural forces at play both inside and outside of the church. For example, if something as simple as a projection screen can have a dynamic effect on a congregational experience in worship, what happens when more complex media are infused into the life of a church or into the lives of the people who are the church? What is the effect of the Internet on the way we think about and do church? How does the medium of television shape our understanding of community, leadership, and mission? In what ways is our understanding of the gospel altered when we communicate or preach with pictures instead of words?

MEDIA: THE CULTURAL ARCHITECT

The answers to these questions are based on a simple notion: The *forms* of media and technology—regardless of their *content*—cause profound changes in the church and culture. The power of our media forms has created both challenges and opportunities in the ways the people of God are formed. Unfortunately, just as Dorothy and her companions missed the man behind the curtain in *The Wizard of Oz*, we stand oblivious to the hidden power of media. Most of us point and stare at the giant wizard head wreathed in flame, quite unaware it is only a distraction—the con man's sleight of hand.

The time has come for the church to pull back the curtain and expose the true effects of media. While this may sound like the hunt for some notorious villain, it is not. The media to which I am referring are neither evil nor good. Yet this in no way means they are neutral. Their power is staggering but remains hidden from view. Because we tend to focus our gaze on their content, the forms of media appear only in our peripheral vision. As a result they exert a subtle yet immense power. By exposing their secrets and powers, we restore our ability to predict and perceive the often unintended consequences of using new media and new methods. This understanding of media is crucial to forming God's people with discernment, authenticity, and faithfulness to the gospel.

MR. NO DEPTH PERCEPTION

In 1991, *Saturday Night Live* introduced America to Mr. No Depth Perception, played by Kevin Nealon. The character made only one appearance, but for some reason the sketch left an indelible mark on my memory. The title tells the story: It's a sketch about an enthusiastic and well-intentioned man who is completely unaware of the fact that he cannot perceive depth or distance in the world.

In the sketch, Mr. No Depth Perception is energized by the prospect of going sky-diving. He imagines how thrilling it must be to "pull the rip cord at just the right moment," only to have his hopes dashed when his wife, for obvious reasons, adamantly refuses to support his eager aspiration. Later he crashes his head through the living room window in a simple attempt to see who is knocking at the door. It happens to be their friend Brenda with her new boyfriend Gary. They sit down for dinner, and Mr. No Depth Perception turns to his wife and says, "I can't believe Brenda's dating this loser! You know what she's after, right?! I bet he's got money or something!" Gary, sitting only a few feet away, fidgets awkwardly in his seat. When Mr. No Depth Perception's wife reprimands him for his insensitivity, he responds by saying, "Oh, relax! He can't hear me way down there!" The sketch goes on like this, but you get the point.

If all comedy is a form of tragedy, then the tragedy for Mr. No Depth Perception is that this rather endearing adult is actually very much a child without any powers of discernment, which means he is quite dangerous to himself and others. As a result he must be tended to and cared for by his family at all times. It makes for good comedy, but it also makes you glad you aren't him.

I find Mr. No Depth Perception to be an appropriate metaphor for the church's relationship to media and technology. We are able to see, but we have great difficulty perceiving. We are able to make observations about what's going on around us, but we often mis-appropriate the meaning of these observations. We recognize that the use of image and icon is fast displacing the written word as the dominant communication system of our culture—a trend easily identified when Nike can strip its name from the swoosh icon without losing an ounce of brand recognition or equity—but we fail to perceive what the new iconic symbol system truly has the capacity to do and undo. We can see the glut of reality TV shows propagating the airwaves, but few understand that these shows reveal more about our understanding of community than our voyeuristic tendencies (something we will discuss later).

Our response to these shifts often stops with simplistic exhortations to either adopt or avoid the torrent of images. We either argue that electronic media have rendered old ways of doing church obsolete or that the new electronic storm is something to be resisted by creating a counterculture. These are not invalid responses; they are simply insufficient.

Like Mr. No Depth Perception, we are quite unaware of the limitations and dangers of our disability, sharing instead in his enthusiasm. Heralding the high virtue of efficiency and effectiveness, we eagerly embrace new media and technologies, assuming they will get the gospel message out better and faster. But prior to making decisions about how to appropriate new media, we must take seriously the role of technology and media in our culture and in the church.

A CULTURE OF ONE-EYED PROPHETS

My concern for the role of media and technology in culture is by no means new. Aside from the many recent cultural commentators who have issued warnings, this subject is also at the center of major films such as *I, Robot; Minority Report;* and *The Matrix*—all of which present apocalyptic visions of social control and the unintended result of technology's power to reverse roles with its creators. In many ways these are merely contemporary retellings of the famous novels of a previous era. George Orwell's *1984* and Aldous Huxley's *Brave New World,* both written before 1950, are prophetic visions of societies overtaken by technological power. Orwell's novel introduces us to the ominous and all-seeing "Big Brother," who is always watching. Orwell warns of a dark and dangerous future where people are forced into conformity by invasive and controlling technology. In contrast, *Brave New World* introduces the critique in a more subtle way; the world Huxley describes promises a seductive, utopian future in which technological promise is the succulent yet poisoned apple.

Humanity's ambivalent relationship with technology has a long history, going back to the early 1800s when the Luddites, a group of mechanics in England, destroyed manufacturing machinery in reaction to the ways in which the technological advances of the Industrial Revolution were replacing human workers. Even earlier, the Amish maintained an equally radical, albeit less violent, rejection of certain technologies. To this day a prohibition on automobiles and electricity is central to the corporate practice of the Amish faith. While such a stance might appear to be an arbitrary time freeze, it is deeply informed by this community's theology of technology.

Even these are not the earliest prophetic warnings about technology. If we turn back time two-and-a-half millennia, we will discover Plato's *Phaedrus,* an account of Socrates instructing a pupil named Phaedrus. Amid the teachings, we learn of a legend that embodies one of the earliest critiques of communication technology in Western history. Socrates tells the story of two Egyptian gods: a king named Thamus and an inventor named Theuth. Theuth is known to have invented, among other things, geometry, arithmetic, astronomy, and writing. Socrates tells Phaedrus:

> Now the king of all Egypt at that time was the god Thamus...To him came Theuth to show his inventions, saying that they ought to be imparted to the other Egyptians.

Thamus inquired into the use of each of them, and as Theuth went through them expressed approval or disapproval, according as he judged Theuth's claims to be well or ill founded. It would take too long to go through all that Thamus is reported to have said for and against each of Theuth's inventions. But when it came to writing, Theuth declared, "Here is an accomplishment, my lord the King, which will improve both the wisdom and the memory of the Egyptians. I have discovered a sure receipt for memory and wisdom." To this, Thamus replied, "Theuth, my paragon of inventors, the discoverer of an art is not the best judge of the good or harm which will accrue to those who practice it. So it is in this; you, who are the father of writing, have out of fondness for your off-spring attributed to it quite the opposite of its real function. Those who acquire it will cease to exercise their memory and become forgetful; they will rely on writing to bring things to their remembrance by external signs instead of by their own internal resources. What you have discovered is a receipt for recollection, not for memory. And as for wisdom, your pupils will have the reputation for it without the reality: they will receive a quantity of information without proper instruction, and in consequence be thought very knowledgeable when they are for the most part quite ignorant. And because they are filled with the conceit of wisdom instead of real wisdom they will be a burden to society. [2]

Thamus is clearly no fan of this new invention of writing; his critique is scathing to say the least.

It may surprise and dishearten some to learn that the Thamus' insights bear striking resemblance to those who warn of the modern dangers of information overload due to television and the Internet. Quentin J. Schultze, author of *Habits of the High-Tech Heart*, describes the Information Age as one in which "…the information explosion will become a plague of *misinformation*—endless volleys of nonsense, folly, rumor masquerading as knowledge, wisdom, and even truth."[3] While Schultze does not cite the ancient legend of Socrates as the source of his analysis, it is as though he took his insightful critique of the Internet straight from the lips of Thamus himself.

In his book *Technopoly* Neil Postman employs the Thamus story to illustrate an important point. King Thamus, who is opposed to writing, and Theuth, who heralds the promise of writing, are both "one-eyed prophets," each with the opposite eye closed.[4] They each present a portion of the truth while simultaneously conveying a subtle error. Thamus has a point: Writing does erode memory, and while it provides for new knowledge, this is in no way equivalent to wisdom. And yet Thamus failed to see the immense advantages of writing.

To perceive the true power and effect of any technology requires us to have both eyes open and to understand technology as Postman understands it—a Faustian bargain that both gives and takes away. This is, of course, hardly a groundbreaking idea. Nonetheless, this simple truth is often forgotten when we are considering the role of new media and technology in the church. I concur with Postman's observation that our culture is teeming with "throngs of zealous Theuths, one-eyed prophets who see only what new technologies can do and are incapable of imagining what they will *undo*."[5] Still, while this is true of our culture at large, it is not quite so simple for the church. Depending upon the denomination, theology, and history of a given church, the positions of both Thamus and Theuth are well represented within today's Christian culture.

To perceive media and technology with both eyes open, we cannot simply list the various benefits and liabilities of all new and existing media in hopes of understanding their power and meaning. Instead, the task before us requires an entirely different approach to analyzing media, recognizing them not simply as conduits or pipelines (i.e., neutral purveyors of information), but rather as dynamic forces with power to shape us, regardless of content. Such an approach invites us to ask different questions, *better* questions, and moves us beyond the oversimplified but common belief that media forms can be deemed good or bad based on how they are used. This perspective is deeply entrenched in the assumption that a medium can be considered "redeemable" if it dispenses the gospel or educational information, but "evil" if it distributes sex and violence. It is imperative we move beyond this paradigm and realize that our forms of media and technology are primary forces that cause changes in our philosophy, theology, culture, and ultimately the way we do church.

PERCEIVING THE POWERS THAT SHAPE US

CHAPTER TWO

In the quotation here Rick Warren reiterates one of the most popular assumptions in the church today: "The methods always change, but the message stays the same." This is the North Star by which the vast majority of Christians have navigated the perpetual changes caused by blustery cultural winds. It guides those who huddle to protect new methods, media, and technologies, all of which have been adopted to amplify the reach and effectiveness of the gospel message. This saying also serves to deflect the attacks of those who cry "Heresy!" whenever a new form is introduced: as long as we hold onto the unchanging gospel message, it doesn't matter what medium or method is used to communicate it.

> "OUR MESSAGE MUST NEVER CHANGE, BUT THE WAY WE DELIVER THAT MESSAGE MUST BE CONSTANTLY UPDATED TO REACH EACH NEW GENERATION."[1]
>
> —RICK WARREN

> "THE MEDIUM IS THE MESSAGE."[2]
>
> —MARSHALL MCLUHAN

Those who espouse this view believe that the primary measuring stick for determining the value of new ministry methods or media is usefulness: How efficient and effective will this new method be? If people are hearing the gospel and responding with decisions for Christ, how can anyone critique this? Such a belief is well intentioned. It is rooted in an authentic desire for the world to know Christ. However, the truth embedded in the second quote at the head of this chapter—"the medium is the message"—reveals the subtle but significant error in the first quote. McLuhan's words tell an important truth: *Whenever methods or media change, the message automatically changes along with them.*

The purpose of this chapter is to help us develop a kind of radar by which to detect the hidden effects of media so we can discern the ways our media and methods are forming God's people. Our guide and teacher for this task will be Marshall McLuhan, the author of the aphorism above. The concepts and precepts laid out in this chapter form the necessary components for developing our radar. This will serve as the central framework for the remaining chapters.

In some ways, this chapter is like learning the rules of football prior to actually playing the game. You get the basics, but it really comes together when the whistle blows and the ball is snapped. Some of these concepts may seem a little foreign, whereas others will put words to what you have intuitively always known. As we move through the subsequent chapters, these ideas will be applied to the church in variety of practical ways. As you see them in action, they will begin to make more sense.

MARSHALL WHO?

This may come as a shock, but aspects of the emerging church were predicted by Marshall McLuhan in the 1960s. McLuhan was fluent in seven languages, held two master's degrees as well as a Ph.D. from Cambridge in English Literature, and received ten honorary doctorates in his lifetime. But more important, between 1965 and 1975 no other figure in popular culture held more sway in the media than Marshall McLuhan. He was so ingrained in the popular vernacular that several entries in the *Oxford English Dictionary* were added under his name ("McLuhanism," "McLuhanesque," and "McLuhanite"). At the height of his popularity he made a cameo in Woody Allen's Academy Award-winning film *Annie Hall.*

In 1967 he became only the second person ever to be the subject of the cover story in *Life* and *Newsweek* in the same week (Barbra Streisand was the other one).[3] *Newsweek* commented that McLuhan's

"…theory of communication offers nothing less than an explanation of all human culture, past, present, and future."[4] In 1969 *Playboy* Magazine featured an extensive interview with McLuhan in which they named him "The High Priest of Popcult and the Metaphysician of Media."[5] But perhaps more than all of this, he was known for his powerful speaking gifts, which sent him on a 10-year tornado tour of TV talk shows and the lecture circuit.

It was an unexpected turn of events that transformed McLuhan from a professor of literature mired in obscurity into a pop culture guru. In 1964 he published *Understanding Media: The Extensions of Man*, and the pundits of cultural study granted it the standing of "Holy Scripture" almost immediately. With absolutely no promotion it became a bestseller. By the fall of 1965 the *New York Herald Tribune* heralded McLuhan as "the most important thinker since Newton, Darwin, Freud, Einstein, and Pavlov…" This was no marginal voice, but rather the consensus of informed opinion at the time.[6] Suddenly, McLuhan was in high demand and thrust into the spotlight. He coined terms like "Global Village" and "Age of Information" decades before the Internet and long before anyone had named the phenomenon of "globalization." Everyone wanted to know what McLuhan was thinking.

He had made more than a few bold cultural predictions—from the rise of the hippie movement to the Internet—years before they emerged. But by the late 1970s, people began to feel that what McLuhan was saying just didn't make sense anymore. His statements such as, "We are moving out of the age of the visual into the age of the aural and tactile," and, "We are the television screen…we wear all mankind as our skin,"[7] left audiences staring blankly back at him with the empty gaze of Homer Simpson. His pithy style of aphorisms, probes, and metaphors became increasingly baffling because McLuhan was peering further into the future than the masses could accept or understand.

Over time his critics grew louder, and eventually his ideas were consigned to the attic of pop culture history, where he became a relic of the '60s. On New Year's Eve of 1980, at the low point of his popularity, McLuhan died of a stroke in his sleep at the age of 69. If that were the end of the story, it would be a sad tale indeed. But it is not the end by any means.

During the years that followed McLuhan's death, the cultural shifts brought about by technology effectively performed CPR on his ideas. By the early '90s innovations like the Internet, cable TV, broadband, cell phones, and e-mail began to reshape global culture in dramatic ways. Many of the changes McLuhan had predicted became clearly observable and took on an eerie familiarity. Suddenly, his once-cryptic statements such as, "One is surrounded by answers, millions of them, moving and mutating at electric speed,"[8] made perfect sense to people surfing and sifting through the information onslaught of the Internet. This led to a humble resuscitation of McLuhan's insights. In 1994 the most elite technological institution in the world, MIT, marked McLuhan's comeback with a reissued 30th anniversary edition of *Understanding Media.* That same year saw the debut of a Broadway musical about his life called *The Medium.* In 1996 McLuhan's ghost decorated the cover of the ultrahip techno magazine *Wired.*[9] In that issue he was anointed the patron saint of the publication and has since been featured several times. McLuhan is making unexpected cameos from beyond the grave, and his words carry significant implications for the church.

McLuhan for the Church

As a devout Catholic, McLuhan often used his cultural commentary as a form of stealth theology, which was profoundly informed by his faith.[10] McLuhan had much to say about the church, but his insights on this subject were largely ignored and rarely heeded. For example, just as the megachurch movement was gaining momentum in the early 1970s, he said, "Christianity—in a centralized, administrative, bureaucratic form—is certainly irrelevant."[11] Most people didn't believe him then, but his prediction is increasingly coming true. While certain corners of the church (i.e., Pentecostals and Anabaptists) have always practiced decentralized leadership, it is now becoming the model in many mainstream evangelical churches. This leadership structure is evident in many emerging churches that are seeking to live out the theology of "the priesthood of all believers" by giving real authority to the businesspeople, students, mothers, and artists who make up the body of Christ. In the process these churches are casting off the bureaucracy to which McLuhan refers. McLuhan was able to predict changes in the church because he understood the power of media and technology to shape nearly everything in their path—even the way institutions are organized.

THE STORY OF THREE SAILORS

To understand how McLuhan developed his insight and prophetic understanding of media's impact on culture—and hopefully deepen our own powers of discernment—it is helpful to begin where he did. If we can start thinking a little more like McLuhan, we will begin to perceive the hidden forces shaping the people of God.

One of McLuhan's favorite metaphors for describing how he came to understand the effects of media was Edgar Allan Poe's short story "A Descent into the Maelstrom," in which Poe tells the story of a fisherman and his brothers who regularly sail the Arctic Ocean off the coast of Norway. Just off the northwest coast, there is an area where fish are just waiting to be caught. However, few sailors dare make this voyage because it demands that they plot a course around a treacherous whirlpool known as the Maelstrom. This dreaded vortex had repeatedly proven its peril, devouring boats, whales, and even the largest ships. But the fisherman and his brothers regularly brave these waters in search of the bounty, risking their lives each time they navigate the perimeter of the black, swirling sea. On two occasions they are even stranded out beyond the Maelstrom and have to anchor overnight.

One day, after several years of making this risky voyage, the brothers are returning to port when a hurricane blows in. Immediately, it begins to batter their boat, driving it directly into the dreaded darkness of the massive whirling waters. In a panic, one of the brothers lashes himself to the mast of the boat for safety, but under the strain of the storm the mast snaps and falls into the sea, dragging him to his death. The other two brothers are carried with their vessel into the Maelstrom.

Amid the tornado of water, one of the brothers sees both horror and wonder. He begins to discern a strange pattern in which certain objects descend quickly to the jagged rocks at the bottom of the vortex and are destroyed whereas other objects defy the laws of gravity and gradually ascend out of the Maelstrom. This pattern gives him hope and a clue to his survival. Due to the whirling chaos and deafening white noise, the sailor is unable to help his brother understand this discovery, so he abandons ship and ties himself to a barrel that gradually pulls him out of the vortex. His brother stays with the vessel, assuming it to be more secure, only to perish when he is sucked under by the force of the current.

The brother who survives is carried down the coast and eventually rescued by old friends who are also fishermen. When he tells of his ordeal and how he managed to escape, they do not believe him.

McLuhan repeatedly employs this story in his writing and teaching as a metaphor for his method. He writes, "Poe's sailor saved himself by studying the action of the whirlpool and by cooperating with it."[12] In a lecture McLuhan said, "The huge vortices of energy created by our media present us with similar possibilities of evasion, of consequences, of destruction. By studying the pattern of the effects of this huge vortex of energy in which we are involved, it may be possible to program a strategy of evasion and survival."[13] In speaking of his own rescue, the survivor in Poe's story could just as easily be speaking for McLuhan when he says, "I became obsessed with the keenest curiosity about the whirl itself. I positively felt a wish to explore its depths, even at the sacrifice I was going to make."[14] McLuhan gained many of his media insights by stepping back and perceiving the broader patterns of the entire "whirl" of media rather than its individual parts. This allowed him to cooperate with the Maelstrom rather than be swept away by it. In the same way we are invited to step back and perceive the power of our media, not in an effort to stop them but, for the purpose of navigating them.

THE MEANING OF MEDIA

Before going any further to explore the specifics of McLuhan's method, it is helpful to clarify the definition of an important word used frequently throughout this book: *media*. The definition I use is taken from the subtitle of McLuhan's book *Understanding Media: The Extensions of Man*. Every medium is an extension of our humanity. This is the starting point for his approach to media and the doorway to understanding their power and meaning.

All forms of media (i.e., any human invention or technology) extend or amplify some part of ourselves. They either extend a part of our body, one or more of the senses, some function of our mental processes, or some social process. For example, the invention of the wheel is an extension of our body in that it amplifies the function of the foot. The telephone extends and amplifies the voice and the ear. Eyeglasses extend the focusing ability of the eye. Weapons, such as guns or knives, are extensions of our teeth and our fists. Even a method of organizing information such as an outline is a medium in that it extends our ability to comprehend complex topics more easily.

This definition is extremely broad and thus a little unusual. Included in this definition are obvious forms such as television, film, and magazines. I will also use it to include communications technologies such as the telegraph, cell phones, e-mail, books, and even the spoken word. But McLuhan uses the word to describe items we don't usually consider media, including all human creations or inventions from cars and clothing to clocks and credit cards.

Understanding media as extensions of ourselves is crucial to understanding media, period. When we fail to see media this way, we become overly enamored, giving them the power to make us slaves to our own creations. This could be something as simple as the stress we feel from needing to respond to the demands of a hundred e-mails when we return from a week away from work. Or it could be our love affair with a brand-new car that presents us with the terrible possibility of its getting a scratch. Perhaps it is simply the incessant cry of the cell phone that can only be comforted when we answer it. But this slavery to our technologies is much more profound than these obvious examples. Consider two ancient stories: One illustrates the danger of our natural tendency to make idols of our gadgets; the other poses the antidote to this upside-down relationship between the creator and the created.

The Problem with Narcissus

As a professor of literature, McLuhan loved poetry, stories, and myth and used them to help explain his ideas—and rightly so. These ancient stories tell important truths about the human condition that transcend time and culture. Central to McLuhan's observations about media and culture was his interpretation of the Greek myth of Narcissus. This story has been classically interpreted as a warning against excessive self-love, but as we will see, McLuhan believed it warned of something quite different.

The myth tells the story of an exceptionally handsome man named Narcissus who was loved by all the maidens in the woods. He never returned their love, so they grew angry and asked the gods to curse Narcissus with the experience of unrequited love. The avenging gods granted the request.

Deep in the woods there was a clear fountain with water that reflected like silver. One day Narcissus stumbled upon the fountain, exhausted and thirsty after a day of hunting. Leaning over to drink, he saw his own image in the mirror of clear water, but he mistook it for a beautiful water spirit living in the fountain. He stood gazing at those bright eyes, curled locks of hair, and the glow of health and immediately fell in love. But when he approached the image for a kiss, it contorted and fled at the point of contact. In time it would return, and he became enamored once more. He was so completely taken by this image in the mirror that he lost all thought of food or rest. Over time he began to starve, but the pain of hunger could not outweigh the power of the stunning beauty that enraptured him. Eventually, he withered away and died.

As I said, the traditional interpretation of this story is that Narcissus fell in love with himself; this is where Freud derived the term *narcissism*, used to describe extreme levels of selfishness and self-interest. But McLuhan took a different stance. In McLuhan's view the chief error of Narcissus was not that he fell in love with himself but rather that he failed to recognize himself in the fountain's reflection. This may seem an unimportant distinction, but it is quite significant for our discussion. Narcissus became "numb" to his own extended image in the low-tech medium of the fountain. He could not perceive that the image was really just an extension of himself and became overly enamored with it, leading to his death. If he had understood that this fountain was simply a mirror reflecting his own face, Narcissus would have been able to dispel the power of the pool and gain control over it. No such luck. As proof of this interpretation, McLuhan points out that the name Narcissus is derived from the Greek word *narcosis*, which means "numbness." Thus Narcissus suffered because he became numb to the technology that came to enslave him.

When we fail to perceive media as extensions of ourselves, they take on godlike characteristics, and we become their servants.[15]

The Solution of Perseus

While McLuhan never referenced the myth of Perseus, it offers a promising solution to the problem encountered by Narcissus regarding the power of media. This myth tells of the young man named Perseus, a son of the god Zeus. In the land where Perseus grew up, a horrifying monster named Medusa was on a rampage; everyone who looked directly into her eyes was immediately turned to stone. Perseus volunteered to find and destroy her.

As Perseus set out for Medusa's lair, the gods gave him a highly polished shield for protection. When Perseus arrived, Medusa was sleeping. Perseus approached quietly, being cautious never to look directly at her. But instead of proceeding with his eyes closed, he used his bright shield as a mirror to guide himself, keeping his eyes fixed on the reflection of Medusa. Suddenly, she awoke with a hiss and glared at Perseus. Because he saw only her reflection in his shield, her gaze had no effect. Immediately, Perseus struck with his sword, shearing off her head. Upon his return Perseus offered Medusa's head as a gift to the king, and there was peace in the land.

In both stories the low-tech medium of a mirror serves as the primary plot point. For Narcissus the fountain mirror was a mysterious and powerful medium he could not understand. He was distracted by the content—his own reflection—and it gained power over him, leading to his death. Perseus, on the other hand, was aware that the mirror was an extension of himself that he could control.[16] This understanding allowed him to survive an ordeal that had claimed the lives of countless others. When we become aware of the specific ways in which technology and media serve as extensions of ourselves, much of their power is dispelled. We are returned to being owners of technology rather than those who are owned by it.

Recently I was having lunch with a friend. As we chatted, his ringing cell phone interrupted nearly every other sentence. "Sorry, I have to get this," he would say. Each time I would wait, and each time he would apologize. The last time it rang, he said with a sense of resignation and exhaustion, "I am a total slave to my cell phone." This experience of being enslaved by a technology is not uncommon and can be quite unnerving. However, when we perceive the cell phone as an extension of ourselves, such a statement becomes senseless; it is like saying, "I am a slave to my ears or my voice"—the very parts of ourselves that the cell phone extends.

Understanding media as extensions of ourselves is crucial to perceiving their hidden power and effects. Equally important is moving beyond another common misconception—that media forms are little more than tools.

THE MEDIUM IS THE MESSAGE

"AT SADDLEBACK, ANY TIME A NEW TOOL COMES DOWN THE LINE, WE EMBRACE IT. RIGHT NOW WE'RE USING TIVO TO BROADCAST OUR WEEKEND SERMON INTO SEVERAL DIFFERENT VENUES ON OUR CAMPUS."[17]

—RICK WARREN

When we talk about media and technology as tools for the church, we assume they are simply conduits or pipelines useful for dispensing the gospel. Thus media become like the plumbing of a house, carrying water from the water heater to the faucet. And we don't think much about the pipes unless one springs a leak.

However, McLuhan's simple yet provocative statement "The medium is the message" issues a direct challenge to this understanding of media. He writes, "Our conventional response to all media, namely that it is how they are used that counts, is the numb stance of the technological idiot. The 'content' of a medium is like the juicy piece of meat carried by the burglar to distract the watchdog of the mind."[18] In other words, media are much more than neutral purveyors of information. They have the power to shape us regardless of content and thus cannot be evaluated solely upon their use. He challenges the pervasive notion that if a medium dispenses violence or sex, it is bad, but if it dispenses the gospel, it is good. In this view, televangelism redeems the medium of TV. But the moment *Desperate Housewives*, with its overt extramarital affairs, homosexual references, drug use, and murder is piped through, the medium is bad. We give little thought to the ways in which the medium of TV itself impacts us.

In truth, the content of a given form of media actually distracts us from detecting the effects of its form. When we watch TV, we are almost completely oblivious to the medium itself. The flickering mosaic of light that creates the images simply washes over us, bypassing our conscious awareness. Instead, we sit hypnotized by the TV show—the content—which has gripped our attention. We are oblivious to the ways the medium, regardless of its content, reduces our capacity for abstract thought, makes us prefer intuition and experience over logic and reasoning, and revives tribal experiences in an individualistic culture.

In the same way, we often fail to consider how preaching with images shapes our message and minds in ways that are completely different from the effects of preaching with words. We miss the power of the Internet to alter the very meaning of truth in our culture. We remain unaware of the way electronic media change the way we interpret Scripture. As we will see, these media forms have a profound effect on our faith—an effect that goes far beyond their content.

McLuhan expresses this idea forcefully: "The content or message of any particular medium has about as much importance as the stenciling on the casing of an atomic bomb."[19] In other words, the medium has far more impact on the culture than its content. As a prophet crying out in the wilderness, McLuhan uses these hyperbolic metaphors to shake us from our state of numbness and slumber.

A MIRROR IN *THE MATRIX*

The Matrix is an amazing commentary on the ways technology can overtake a culture. There is a pivotal scene in the film where the protagonist, Neo, is about to get an answer to his long-asked question, "What is the matrix?" Morpheus, the prophetic guide, has taken Neo into a secret room and asked Neo to be seated in a chair. Neo anxiously awaits the big revelation. But something strange happens that diverts his attention. To Neo's right is a cracked mirror (our favorite symbol returns!), which reflects a fractured image of himself. As Neo looks at the mirror, the cracks suddenly begin to recede and bleed together, making the mirror whole again. Neo's reflection is no longer fractured, and he is startled. The move from a cracked mirror to a whole one foreshadows the clarity Neo is about to receive concerning the technology that has imprisoned him.

Doing a double take, Neo asks if this is a dream. He begins to study the mirror rather than his reflection. He reaches out to touch it, but at the point of contact it bends and bows like liquid mercury, then snaps plumb again around his fingers. Neo quickly recoils from this strange medium, but a portion of the mysterious mirror adheres to his fingers and rapidly multiplies until it begins to consume him. Immediately, we cut to Neo trapped in an incubation pod, struggling to escape. From here he is born into the "real world," and the whole story turns in a new direction. There is no going back.

In this case, the mirror is a metaphor for the technological world of the Matrix. At first the mirror appears rather harmless, but suddenly, it takes on a life of its own. In the same way, the world the humans created in the film was initially benign but eventually took on a life of its own and enslaved the whole human race.

When Neo studies the medium of the mirror instead of being distracted by his reflection—its content—he is freed from the prison of his mind; it is only when he observes the medium apart from its content that he perceives its true power. With this discovery he is awakened from his numbness and slumber. Like Morpheus, McLuhan wants to free our minds by studying the medium, not just the message.

It may appear as if I'm arguing that content doesn't matter. This is not the case. Yet I do believe we too often focus only on the content and ignore the medium. To truly understand the power of media, we have to understand the relationship between the two.[20] To focus exclusively on one or the other is like trying to drive a car with wheels but no axles.[21]

THE ECOLOGY OF MEDIA

As we begin to perceive the power of the medium regardless of the message, we soon discover that the metaphor of media forms as conduits or containers is not adequate. Instead, it is more helpful to borrow a principle from the environmental science of ecology. The principle of ecology refers to the ways in which environments change and adapt. For example, imagine two adjacent rooms separated by a wall. In one room the temperature is 20 degrees; in the adjacent room the temperature is 90 degrees. If the dividing wall is removed, the two temperatures are blended to form a completely new climate. In the same way, communication media often serve to remove the walls of time and distance. As a result, formerly separate worlds collide, creating entirely new cultural ecologies.

Electronic culture has broken down major walls as we extend ourselves in a global embrace. Under these conditions, the world undergoes a kind of implosion; the barriers of time and space are abolished, greatly diminishing the scale of our world—which leads to the phenomenon of the Global Village. As we will see in the chapters ahead, this has a profound effect on the way we as Christians practice community and imagine our mission in the world.

THE LAWS OF MEDIA

While these changes are often difficult to detect, McLuhan believed the effect of any medium could be anticipated if we simply asked the right questions. He developed what he called The Laws of Media,[22] a set of questions designed to tune us in to what he believed to be the four inevitable effects of all media. These are the four questions we will be asking in different ways as we seek to discern our culture and the true power and effects of media.

What does the medium **extend***?* You'll recall that McLuhan believed every new medium enhances, amplifies, or extends some human capacity. Determining which part of ourselves—and this might be a body part (the camera is an extension of the eye), a previous medium (the telephone is an extension of the telegraph), or even an emotion (smoke detectors extend our sense of smell as well as our feeling of security)—is extended is essential to understanding the ways in which that medium impacts society.

What does the medium make **obsolete***?* Every new medium makes an older technology obsolete. In this case the word *obsolete* does not necessarily mean the technology has disappeared but that the function of that previous medium has changed. For example, the automobile made the horse and buggy obsolete. This means the horse and buggy went from being used for transportation to being used for quaint entertainment and romance.

What does the medium **reverse into***?* This is the law where we discover the dangers of media. When pushed to its extreme, every medium will reverse into its opposite intention. For example, when pushed to the extreme, the automobile—a medium intended to increase the speed of transportation—reverses into traffic jams and fatal accidents. This law of reversal can often be the most difficult to predict or anticipate. But sometimes the answer to the following question sheds light on this effect.

What does the medium **retrieve***?* Every new medium retrieves some ancient experience or medium from the past. In other words, there is no such thing as a completely new technology. When we discover which medium is retrieved, we can study its effects in hindsight in an effort to anticipate the future of the new medium. For example, the medium of e-mail retrieves the telegraph. If we want to understand the future effects of e-mail, we would be wise to study the cultural effects of the telegraph in the 1800s.

To demonstrate how we can apply McLuhan's four laws to the media forms available to the church, let's use them to assess the technology of something that, while ubiquitous in most urban settings, often goes completely unnoticed: surveillance cameras.

THE LAWS OF MEDIA
APPLIED TO SURVEILLANCE CAMERAS

A surveillance camera extends the capacity of the human eye and enhances the feeling of security and "eyewitness" accounts.

When pushed to the extreme, surveillance cameras reverse into an invasive loss of privacy and a new feeling of vulnerability.

ENHANCES  **REVERSES INTO**

RETRIEVES **OBSOLESCES**

Surveillance cameras retrieve the medieval city wall, which both protected and imprisoned its citizens.

A surveillance camera makes obsolete (or changes the function of) neighborhood watch groups and oral testimony.

FIGURE 1

This is not intended as a definitive set of answers to these questions—you can probably think of others. The point is not always to find the conclusive answer to each question. On the contrary, the real power comes from simply asking the questions and probing the situation.

New questions serve to move our minds beyond traditional ways of thinking. This is why McLuhan framed his Laws of Media as questions rather than statements. This is not an analytic activity but one that demands creativity, synthesis, and openness. Our media present us with an array of questions and no clear answers. McLuhan knew our cultural context was always changing, so the methods he used to investigate and analyze culture were quite unconventional. Decades ago he said:

> In a global information environment, the old pattern of education in answer finding is one of no avail...Survival and

control will depend on the ability to probe and to question in the proper way and place…the need is not for fixed concepts but rather for the ancient skill of navigating through an ever uncharted and unchartable milieu. Else we will have no more control of this technology and environment than we have of the wind and the tides.[23]

We are being invited to develop and hone the ancient skill of "navigating through an ever uncharted and unchartable" culture. This skill is not developed through finding the right answers and locking onto fixed ideas but rather by having the courage and wisdom to ask the right questions at the right times and places.

In the next two chapters we will apply this new perspective on media and technology to the story of Western culture and the church. Specifically, we will see how major changes in media and technology caused seismic shifts in culture and shaped the people of God in hidden ways. The lessons of these stories are intended to help us develop discernment for our current situation.

PRINTING: THE ARCHITECT OF THE MODERN CHURCH

CHAPTER THREE

APPLYING MCLUHAN'S MESSAGE...ER, MEDIUM

Perhaps we can best understand the ways in which the medium and the message are intertwined by examining the effects of a technology so familiar it is rarely considered a technology. It is the one you are consuming right now: the printed word. But this study of print is more than an exercise. I contend the medium of print shaped the modern church in ways we are only beginning to recognize in the wake of postmodernism. Only when we study these changes can we begin to perceive the impact of the other forms of media on our understanding of community, leadership, and worship.

> "THE PRINTED BOOK ADDED MUCH TO THE NEW CULT OF INDIVIDUALISM. THE PRIVATE, FIXED POINT OF VIEW BECAME POSSIBLE AND LITERACY CONFERRED THE POWER OF DETACHMENT, NONINVOLVEMENT."[1]
>
> —MARSHALL MCLUHAN

DYSLEXIA AND DECEPTION

The medium of the printed word is one I have learned not to take for granted. When I was in the second grade, we were often subjected to timed, in-class reading tests. I was convinced those tests were from Satan. They required me to muster every last brain cell to decipher the words and sentences on the page. After straining through the first couple of sentences, I would inevitably notice that the two students sitting to my right and left had already gone on to the next page while I was still stuck on the first paragraph. A panic would set in, and I found myself turning the page whenever they did so I wouldn't look dumb or slow. It seemed like a good plan at the time. Of course we were often quizzed on the material we had just read (or in my case, not read), and needless to say I did not score well. Naturally, it didn't take long for my teachers and parents to catch on.

When it became clear my poor performance was the rule and not the exception, my parents had me tested for learning disabilities. I was diagnosed with dyslexia—an amorphous condition often caricatured as reading words backward. My dyslexia was a bit more subtle; every time I looked at the printed page, I felt like I had just walked out of a dark movie theater into the bright light of day. It took time for my eyes to adjust and cobble together the letters on the page so I could make sense of them. My biggest problem was leaving out entire words like *not* or *but,* words crucial for comprehension. I would also unknowingly change words that looked similar—*what* might become *when.* By the end of a paragraph I could not make head nor tail of what I had read and would have to go back to the beginning. During my senior year of high school I was tested again and learned I had the reading comprehension of an eighth grader. Since then things have gotten better, but the general struggle remains.

My difficulties with reading and writing didn't just affect my schoolwork. Dyslexia truly makes my brain function differently from the brains of others. In those early diagnostic tests I scored very low on both visual perception and the ability to organize information or objects. That meant that in addition to my reading difficulties, my desk at school was a hopeless mess, a black hole for most of my homework assignments. In contrast, those without difficulty reading had no trouble with visual perception and could organize information and objects with ease. Whether they chose to be organized was a different matter—the point is they had a competence I did not.

At the same time, compared to normal readers, I scored extremely high in the area of short-term memory. This phenomenon is not uncommon among children with dyslexia or other reading problems. The explanation is quite simple: like a blind person who develops acute hearing for survival, my brain compensated for my visual deficits by enhancing memory, specifically auditory memory. Because I could barely access information through the visual act of reading, I depended upon retaining what the teacher said for my learning. Incidentally, as I have become more fluent in the world of literacy, my organizational skills have improved, and my short-term memory has diminished.

My personal experience illustrates a major premise of this chapter: the technology of writing, which relies so heavily on the visual sense, shapes the way we think, regardless of what is written. That fact that I didn't read or write much made me a very different thinker, a different person. What was true for me on an individual level is true on a cultural level as well. The broad introduction of literacy into an entire culture completely alters the way that culture thinks. Writing has the power to restructure the worldview of an entire society. As we shall see, it clearly had that effect on the church.

Of all the media inventions in history, few can rival the explosive and dramatic effects of the written word. This is important to understand, because it shows us that "we become what we behold."[2] That is to say, our thinking patterns begin to mirror the specific form of media we use to communicate.

While we in the West think very little about the power of the written word, those who have lived or worked in purely oral cultures know that the written word holds a magical and mysterious quality for those who have never experienced it before. Consider the experience of a West African tribal prince named Modupe who recounts in his autobiography his first encounter with the mysterious medium of writing:

> The one crowded space in Father Perry's house was his bookshelves. I gradually came to understand that the marks on the pages were trapped words. Anyone could learn to decipher the symbols and turn the trapped words loose again into speech. The ink of the print trapped the thoughts; they could no more get away than a doomboo could get out of a pit. When the full realization of what this meant flooded over me, I experienced the same thrill and amazement as when I had my first glimpse of the bright lights of Konakry [sic]. I shivered with the intensity of my desire to learn to do this wondrous thing myself.[3]

While some of the cultural metaphors are lost on me (I have no idea what a *doomboo* is or where Konakry might be), the point he makes is clear. In fact, I could replace the reference to writing in the paragraph above with a reference to the Internet, and it would reflect well my own enthusiasm when I first encountered this amazing technology.

Writing is not often thought of as a technology. We certainly don't consider it in the same league as the Internet or cell phones. Yet writing is a technology, because it depends upon the use of special tools such as a pen and paper or brushes and animal skins. But more than this, it requires the human invention of a symbol system, one that can take years to learn how to decode (read) and encode (write).[4]

A QUANTUM LEAP: THE PHONETIC ALPHABET

The printing press had been in existence in China for nearly 800 years prior to its European debut in the 1400s, and yet it had none of the same liberating intellectual effects it had in the West.[5] While the Chinese used pictorial writing, the West developed a phonetic alphabet. This may seem like an obscure distinction, but it has far-reaching implications. It is the basis for the hemispheric difference between Eastern and Western worldviews. Understanding this will give us insight into why the postmodern worldview came about in the West and one reason postmodernity shares so much in common with Eastern modes of thinking.

Ideographic writing (e.g., Chinese characters) is distinct from phonetic writing (e.g., the English alphabet) in that it symbolizes spoken language in a completely unique way. Ideographic writing systems, which existed thousands of years prior to phonetic alphabets, are pictorial in nature. A single symbol or character represents an entire word or concept and often bears a resemblance to the thing it describes. For example, the Chinese character for *man* looks like a stylized stick figure of a man (see Figure 2).

PHONETIC WRITING	IDEOGRAPHIC WRITING
man	夫

FIGURE 2

Because each symbol represents an entire word or idea, a dizzying number of characters are required for communication. In fact, that number could be infinite or at least equal to the number of words in the language. The Chinese dictionary has over 80,000 characters and is still growing.[6] The idea of using a printing press for mass communication in China made about as much sense as creating a computer keyboard with 80,000 keys.

The phonetic alphabet, comprised of just over two dozen characters (in the case of English), changed everything. Instead of inventing symbols that corresponded with specific words or ideas, the people who formed phonetic alphabets made meaningless characters that corresponded to meaningless "phonemes" or vocal sounds.[7] For example, the symbol "t" corresponds to the meaningless sound "teh." These symbols are then assembled sequentially to re-create the sound of the spoken word. In other words, the phonetic alphabet is a symbol system that is totally abstracted from reality. Unlike Chinese, the English word *man* looks nothing like a man; it is just a collection of abstract, meaningless squiggly shapes used to create meaning.

Moreover, a phonetic alphabet demands letters be organized in a specific linear sequence in order for them to be meaningful. The collection of symbols a, m, and n doesn't mean anything until it is arranged as m-a-n. By contrast, a single Chinese symbol can stand alone and carry full meaning. While a phonetic alphabet is linear, sequential, and abstract, ideographic writing is nonlinear, holistic, and intuitive.

These two media have very different forms that contribute to the fundamental differences between Eastern and Western approaches to philosophy. Ever since the Greeks perfected the phonetic alphabet, Western philosophy has been centered on linear, fragmented, and sequential forms of logic called syllogisms that perfectly mirror the form of our writing system. In contrast the nonlinear, holistic nature of Eastern philosophy can be summarized by a single symbol, the *yin-yang*, which mirrors ideographic writing.

Figure 3 on the following page summarizes this difference to show us that we become what we behold.

	WESTERN THINKING BASED ON THE SYLLOGISM	EASTERN THINKING BASED ON THE YIN-YANG
WRITING SYSTEM	m-a-n ↓	夫 ↓
PATTERN OF THINKING	All philosophers are men; all men are mortal; therefore, all philosophers are mortal.	
	Notice that the linear, sequential order of logic mirrors the pattern of the Western alphabet.	Notice that the holistic, intuitive nature of the yin-yang mirrors the ideographic writing of the East.

FIGURE 3

It may appear that we have ventured a long way from the church in this exploration, but understanding the distinction matters for us today. In our current culture we are increasingly communicating with images and icons. We need to understand what happens to Western culture when we begin to communicate using images and logos rather than phonetic words, as in the case of Nike.

One consequence is that people in Western culture start thinking more like those in the East. The holistic, intuitive, and experiential emphases of postmodernity (a Western phenomenon) are Eastern in character. So it is worth our while to dig into the ways in which both cultural perspectives have been formed—and re-formed—through media. We will explore the implications of this re-formation for the church more fully in Chapter Four.

PRINTING: IGNITING THE ALPHABET

The formation of the phonetic alphabet was an important element in shaping Western thought, but its true impact became apparent only after it was channeled through the medium of print. Printing amplified the effects of the alphabet with exponential force and completely restructured the culture—and therefore the church—in the process.

The Greeks created their version of the phonetic alphabet around 700 B.C. and had mastered it by 400 B.C.[8] Like a slow gas leak lasting 1,000 years, the alphabet gradually infiltrated Western culture. However, this leak was all but turned off during the fourth century when papyrus supplies dried up, literacy rates plummeted, and Europe returned to a dominantly oral culture. In turn, the medieval Catholic Church began reflecting the characteristics of oral culture, leading to their increasingly mystical and sacramental theology. Literacy was reintroduced to the West in the 12th century when Chinese traders brought paper to Europe.

In the 15th century, Johannes Gutenberg found an innovative use for a wine press, and the modern age of the printing press was born. With this simple invention, Gutenberg unknowingly set off an explosion of such overwhelming power that we continue to feel its reverberations today. Printing made the alphabet perfectly uniform and infinitely repeatable. This mass production placed literacy into the hands of everyone, subsequently launching the Protestant Reformation.

Immediately following the introduction of the printing press in Europe, something unusual happened: nothing. From the 15th century until the early 19th century, no new communication technologies were introduced to alter the way information was carried. As a result, Western culture had more than 400 years to get accustomed to the printed word.[9] By the 17th century, the medium had become the dominant means of communication. These conditions embedded the bias of the printed medium deeply into the Western worldview and gave rise to the modern mindset that represented a dramatic departure from medieval European thought. This newly entrenched worldview was characterized by a strong emphasis on individualism, objectivity, abstraction, and reason, in contrast to the medieval worldview characterized by an emphasis on tribal, mystical, and sacramental experiences.

In some ways this might not seem like a new argument. These dramatic changes in philosophy and religion have long been attributed to the printing press and its role in the unprecedented distribution of new ideas to the masses.[10] But it is rarely understood that these changes were caused more by the form of the printed word than by its content.

In fact, the majority of ideas being disseminated in print were not new at all. In the 200 years following the introduction of the printing press, well over half of all printed books were medieval or ancient manuscripts.[11] The public had a voracious appetite for classical thinkers. Even Martin Luther's ideas borrowed heavily from Augustine's fourth-century theology and the ideas of the 12th-century Waldensians. In spite of this recycling of medieval ideas the form of communication during the age of printing caused the medieval worldview to dissipate and a modern worldview to emerge. Let me show you what I mean.

Mr. Subliminal

In addition to Mr. No Depth Perception, Kevin Nealon played another character on *Saturday Night Live* who illustrates an important truth about media—Mr. Subliminal. Once again the name tells the story: Mr. Subliminal has a unique power to persuade and manipulate people by whispering subliminal messages under his breath, frequently conveying the opposite of his explicit message. In one sketch, Mr. Subliminal is sitting at a bar, talking with the bartender.

> **Mr. Subliminal:** A beer, please.
>
> **Bartender:** All right, sir, here's your beer.
>
> **Mr. Subliminal:** Thanks, partner *(on the house)*. That was quick *(on the house)*. What do I owe you?
>
> **Bartender:** Uh, forget about it. On the house!
>
> **Mr. Subliminal:** Oh? Thank you very much! Hey, you know something *(free cash)*? This is a real classy place *(free cash)*. First time I've been here.
>
> **Bartender:** Oh, I'm glad you like it. I've been working here for years.
>
> **Mr. Subliminal:** Oh, no kidding *(free cash)*? That's great!
>
> **Bartender:** [opens cash register and drops cash on the counter] Here ya go.
>
> **Mr. Subliminal:** What's this for?
>
> **Bartender:** It's free cash; take it.
>
> **Mr. Subliminal:** No, really *(your wallet)*. I can't take this cash *(your wallet)*. I mean, what would I do with it?
>
> **Bartender:** Well, don't be ridiculous! [drops his wallet on the counter] Here, take my wallet—you can put it in there!
>
> **Mr. Subliminal:** Well, okay, if you insist!

Mr. Subliminal has an enviable talent of using subliminal messages to control people without their knowing it. As we shall see, the printed word has the strange power to perform similar manipulations. Regardless of what is being communicated, the printed word quietly whispers subliminal messages *(you're an individual)*. The subject matter could *(you are objective)* be anything. Regardless of the content, we are *(think abstractly)* powerfully shaped by the form *(think rationally)* of the words alone. These messages of printing caused a cultural shift and an emphasis on the individual, on objectivity, on abstract thinking, on rationality, that—for better or worse—came to dominate nearly every aspect of social, political, and religious life during the modern era.

We could spend a whole chapter—or 10—studying the ways in which the printed word shaped modern culture, but that's for another book. Suffice it to say, print was the archetype for nearly every kind of mechanization that followed. By creating the first uniformly repeatable commodity, print became the first assembly line for mass production.[12] This linear, sequential form of visual organization was the basis for the Industrial Revolution and the subsequent methods of mass production used to make everything from cars to fast food. While all of this is worth understanding, for our purposes we will limit our investigation to four primary ways in which printing created the modern church.

PRINT MADE US MORE INDIVIDUALISTIC

In a predominantly oral culture, one in which communication is based on face-to-face oral speech, there is no means for storing information or knowledge outside of the mind. As a result, once knowledge is obtained, the culture depends upon the community to both retain and repeat that knowledge. With the introduction of writing, people are afforded the luxury to learn and think in isolation without the threat of losing those thoughts. As writing becomes the dominant communication system, people no longer need the community to retain teachings, traditions, or identity. As a result, they spend greater amounts of time reflecting in private. This increased isolation creates a new emphasis on individualism. Prior to the written word, a person's identity was completely bound to the tribe; the notion of the individual didn't exist. Because writing introduced the notion of the autonomous self, printing obliterated tribal bonds and profoundly amplified individualism.[13]

This rise of individualism led to an interest in the more personal aspects of faith. Writing allowed Christians to externalize and freeze the dynamic and fleeting inner life of thoughts and feelings. This had a remarkable cooling effect and provided distance from the emotional life.

This isn't all bad. One of writing's greatest gifts to us is the invitation to self-reflection. It created new spiritual practices such as personally reading Scripture, times of solitude, and prayer journaling. By contrast, oral cultures lack the ability to gain distance from themselves or others, which leads to a spirituality that is nearly void of self-reflection and the intimacy of a personal relationship with God.

Still, this shift from the tribe or community to the individual changed the way the church thought about the gospel. The modern age conceived of a gospel that matters primarily for the individual.[14] The gospel was reduced to forgiveness as a transaction, a concern for personal morality, and the intellectual pursuit of doctrinal precision. In this view the Bible became little more than an individual's handbook for moral living and right thinking. As a result, printing had a tendency to erode the communal nature of faith. The church community became little more than a collection of discrete individuals working on their personal relationships with Jesus. The church became "a thousand points of light" and lost sight of the church as the body of Christ—a living, breathing entity, the essence of which depends on the binding interdependence of God's people.

In college my faith was nurtured in a distinctly conservative modern context. I attended a university in Fort Worth, Texas, and vividly recall hearing a famous local pastor speak about Christian discipleship. We all sat with pens and notebooks in hand, furiously scribbling down his every word. He finished his talk with the following statement: "I've never met a godly man who hasn't had a quiet time every morning!" Most of us in the room found that to be a reasonable and worthy goal and nodded in affirmation. In this view the life of faith can be distilled down to daily quiet times— individual time spent reading Scripture, journaling, and praying in an effort to get the right thoughts in your head and live a moral day.

Over time I've come to see a basic flaw in this viewpoint. Of course these disciplines are immensely valuable for a life of faith; the problem is not the practices themselves, but rather where we rank them. In this case these highly individualistic disciplines were placed above everything else as the primary means to discipleship. The pastor's teaching (and my enthusiasm for it) expresses one of the great consequences of printing's bias toward individualism. It leads to the belief that the church exists primarily for improving my individual relationship with Jesus. Faith then moves from being personal to being private, a shift that is antithetical to the biblical understanding of what it means to live as God's people.

PRINT INTRODUCED THE NOTION OF OBJECTIVITY

The modern mind is very fond of objectivity. It wants very much to think about ideas like truth and belief in such a way that personal, subjective interpretation is ruled out. This way of thinking is a direct result of the technology of writing and printing, which separates the knower from the knowledge. For the first time people were able to stand outside their ideas and observe them on a printed page. This detachment had a profound effect, as it introduced the belief that we can stand outside something and judge it. In oral cultures, where there is no way to separate oneself from one's ideas, the notion of objectivity almost never emerges.

This objectivity isn't necessarily bad. The benefit to our faith is that objectivity temporarily frees us from the amorphous and tumultuous world of subjective experience by allowing us to get outside ourselves. It enables us to step back and observe situations from a distance, thereby gaining a stabilizing perspective on both ideas and relationships. The distance afforded by printing gives us the ability to act without reacting. When I am angry at someone and I take time to journal my feelings or write an e-mail without sending it, I am able to gain distance, calm down, and return to the situation with a new perspective. When I read something I'm not sure I agree with, I can stand outside the experience of reading it and ponder the idea—something that's difficult to do in a spoken conversation.

However, when objectivity is taken to its extreme, it leads to the belief that we can read and discover biblical truths with an unbiased clarity of vision. We presume the Bible presents an objective set of propositions that everyone will discover if they just read it properly. This inflated sense of objectivity, fueled by printing, breeds an unfortunate and arrogant illusion of omniscience. It leaves little room for subjective experience and the work of the Holy Spirit.

Subjective experience is inescapable. Whether I know it or even like it, I read the Bible through the inescapable lenses of a privileged white American male who was raised in a Midwestern suburb. My reading of Scripture will be vastly different from that of a Latin American woman struggling in destitute poverty under the oppressive rule of a dictatorship. The subjective experience of our social location, among other things, has a tendency to magnify certain parts of Scripture while masking the importance of others.

This may sound like a descent into meaningless relativism, but it isn't. The fact that our subjective experiences color the way we read Scripture isn't a surprise to God. That's part of the beauty and mystery of Scripture. The stories of the Bible are remarkably adaptable to speaking to people in divergent contexts. We must remember that the Bible is not merely a collection of objective propositions. It is largely a story told through hundreds of different perspectives and diverse social settings. The mere fact that the Bible includes four versions of the life of Jesus tells us that subjective experience and interpretation have places in a life of faith.

When print dominates, we lose awareness of our subjectivity. Yet our subjective selves—our experiences, our perceptions, our personal histories—are where Christ meets us in our daily lives. Without a level of subjectivity, the Bible remains a set of abstract and distant propositions. The typographical bias toward objectivity is very valuable, but it has a tendency to erode both our humanity and our humility.

PRINT MADE US THINK MORE ABSTRACTLY

In an oral culture, once knowledge is acquired, it has to be continually repeated, or it will be lost. As a result, communication and thought patterns tend to be conservative, redundant, highly formulaic, and related to practical or concrete matters. Such patterns are essential for retaining wisdom and effective administration. Printing introduced a new way to store knowledge that no longer depended upon fixed mnemonic formulas and repetition. This freed the mind for more original and abstract thought.[15] People were no longer bound by the pragmatic concern of retention and were free to think in more creative ways. But oral cultures, not possessing the ability to freeze words in space, find intellectual abstraction and creativity of little use, for these only serve to weaken their most central memories, traditions, and corporate identity. And keep in mind: the alphabet is a collection of shapes that have no basis in reality—phonetic writing is an abstract medium. This simple attribute alone leads to a preference for abstract matters.

Here again, this shift in perception and understanding caused the approach to theology and faith to become more abstract as well. Prior to the rise of printing, worship was centered on the concrete practices of the sacraments, like baptism or communion. But with the new capacity and enthusiasm for abstract thought due to printing, the pulpit began to displace the altar and sacraments, like communion or baptism. Preaching became the high point of the worship service in the modern Protestant church. Moreover, modern sermons became extremely abstract, lengthy, and dense.

Consider the preaching of 18th-century evangelists. Theologian Jonathan Edwards often preached sermons that lasted up to four hours.[16] George Whitefield, a contemporary of Edwards, preached one sermon entitled "A Preservative Against Unsettled Notions, and Want of Principles, in Regard to Righteousness and Christian Perfection."[17] The title alone reveals the tremendous preference for complex, abstract thinking during the age of print; it sounds more like a doctoral dissertation than a sermon. Move beyond the title, and you will discover that it is written with the same complex reasoning, lengthy sentence construction, and dense technical language characteristic of an academic paper.

You might presume these sermons were intimidating for the common audience. On the contrary, these were the great revival sermons of the day. Edwards and Whitefield were to the 18th century what Billy Graham was to the 20th century. Their sermons were so influential they became the primary force behind the Great Awakening, which gave birth to the modern evangelical movement in America.[18] While these preachers had great intellect, their influence also reveals something about the nature of their audiences. I don't know anyone today who could withstand a four-hour dissertation reading, let alone be moved to tears and convert on the spot. But in a culture so thoroughly shaped by the abstract nature of the printed word, those 18th-century audiences not only had the capacity to receive these sermons, but they also preferred such sermons.

Another effect of this emphasis on abstraction was that Protestants became preoccupied with getting their doctrine straight. Anyone who didn't hold a particular set of abstract propositions in her head was deemed a heretic. As the modern age of print continued,

Christians began scanning the Bible to extract propositional truths from disparate places and contexts in order to organize their theology into abstract categories. This became known as "systematic theology," a chief resource of the modern age and one that continues to be a core curriculum in most seminaries today. The benefit of systematic theology is that it helps us discover and create a coherent system of beliefs about the nature of Jesus, the church, and God—beliefs that shape the way we interact with the world. Taken to its extreme, as in the modern period, abstract thinking becomes detached from the needs of the world and the church. In many cases systematic theology has become an obscure discipline that rarely finds itself useful outside the walls of academia. In fact, a professor of systematic theology I know once remarked with pride that the discipline is only intended for academic concerns, not practical ones.

PRINT INTENSIFIES LINEAR, RATIONAL THINKING

As noted above, a phonetic alphabet is relentlessly linear and demands the sequential arrangement of otherwise meaningless symbols. It facilitates modes of thinking that reflect and value the same linear, sequential pattern. Printing amplified and greatly extended this symbol system, leading to modernity's Age of Reason, in which linear, rational thought came to be the sole means of discovering truth. In the life of faith, the reasoning skills fostered by print extend our capacity for discernment. They strengthen our ability to use abstract logic, an essential skill in understanding the meaning of Scripture, among other things. For example, without these skills the letters of Paul are nearly inaccessible.

Paul was a highly literate person, and his letters reflect the kind of abstract if/then reasoning characteristic of a literate mind. This sits in contrast to the gospels, which are characterized by concrete storytelling rooted in the oral tradition. Prior to printing, medieval culture accessed Scripture largely through stained glass windows, which were well-suited to present the life of Jesus but were hard-pressed to articulate the dense theological reasoning of Paul's letters. The printing press not only provided an appropriate medium for Paul's message, but it also helped modern culture develop the reasoning skills necessary to comprehend his message. This is one reason why Martin Luther's rediscovery of Romans resonated with post-Reformation culture in a way it couldn't have before that point.

However, just as with the other effects of printing discussed here, problems arose when linear reasoning was pushed to the extreme, becoming the primary means of determining truth. This led to a belief that the gospel could be established and received only through reason and facts. When this belief became fully absorbed into the cultural bloodstream, we began to view the unknown as a threat, an enemy to be conquered. This undermined our willingness to appreciate and accept mystery, a crucial element of faith. Furthermore, because the printed word demands such intense cognitive processing, it tends to atrophy the value of the intuitive and emotional life. It makes us suspicious and occasionally even fearful of feelings as they relate to faith. This is one reason why the often-unbidden charismatic outbursts of the Great Awakenings were repudiated, even by Edwards and Whitefield.[19]

The modern preference for linear reasoning and suspicion of feelings is also well illustrated by "The Four Spiritual Laws," an evangelistic tract by the late Bill Bright. In this pamphlet, Bright laid out the syllogism of four abstract propositions one must believe in order to be saved. Once the doctrines have been believed through reason and Christ is accepted through cognitive assent, Bright issues a stark warning under the heading "Do Not Depend on Feelings." What follows is a well-known train diagram and subsequent explanation. (Notice that the linear, sequential arrangement of the diagram directly mirrors the form of the printed word.)

FIGURE 4

The train will run with or without a caboose. However, it would be useless to attempt to pull the train by the caboose. In the same way, as Christians we do not depend on feelings or emotions, but we place our faith (trust) in the trustworthiness of God and the promises of his Word.[20]

The bias of printing is deeply embedded in this articulation of the gospel. The relegation of emotion to the caboose is unfortunate, for it reduces our view of people to little more than cognitive, rational beings. Such a belief has a tendency to repress and devalue the emotional or intuitive aspects of our humanity. This directly contradicts the truth and model of the Psalms, which reveal that the emotional life is integral to worship, God's character, and our very being (as evidenced by Psalms 6, 13, 102, 103, and countless others). There is a holistic and interpenetrating relationship between our intellect, volition, and feelings. Scripture does not suggest a hierarchy among these elements of the human spirit.

PERCEIVING PRINT: APPLYING THE FOUR LAWS OF MEDIA

There are a host of other attributes to describe modernity and the cultural effects of the printing press. But for our purposes, I have limited this investigation to these four, for I believe they have the greatest significance for the church. Like all media, the printed word presents us with gains and losses. In an effort to codify and summarize these discoveries and their effect on the Christian faith, McLuhan's Four Laws diagram is a useful tool.

The Four Laws of Media

THE EFFECTS OF PRINTING ON CHRISTIANITY

Printing amplifies the notion of a personal relationship with God. It nurtures individual spiritual practices. It enhances our capacity for discerning Scripture through critical reason and analysis.

When printing is taken to an extreme, we reduce the gospel to a gospel for one and turn it into a set of abstract propositions to be believed. It also creates the illusion that we can see truth with perfect objectivity.

ENHANCES

REVERSES INTO

RETRIEVES

OBSOLESCES

Printing retrieved Paul's epistles for the church. The stained glass windows used prior to print were ill suited to convey the abstract and highly rational prose of Paul.

Printing has a tendency to obsolesce (or change the function of) communal faith. In addition, it erodes the intuitive aspects of faith along with our appreciation for mystery.

FIGURE 5

The answers offered here trace only a few contours of the effects of print. I encourage you to explore other associations and stimulate your own new connections; remember, these queries are nearly inexhaustible.

Like all technologies, the printing press presents us with gains and losses. Some are more significant than others, but the medium is in no way neutral. Some of these effects have been useful aids to the gospel, while others have left a legacy that has limited our understanding of the Good News. This perspective is not a call to become desperate or alarmed by these deeper effects of printing. Instead, our understanding of its power should help us employ the printed word with an intentionality that respects its subliminal messages.

ELECTRONIC MEDIA: PLANTING THE SEEDS OF THE EMERGING CHURCH

CHAPTER FOUR

It could be said the emerging church began in 1832 on a voyage across the Atlantic Ocean when a struggling artist named Samuel F. B. Morse sailed aboard a ship from England to America. It was then that he first became enamored by the possibility of communicating using electricity. Twelve years later, on May 24, 1844, Morse established the very first electric communication, which was sent between Baltimore and Washington, D.C. His now famous—and quite prophetic—inaugural message exclaimed simply, "What hath God wrought?"[3] That same year the German philosopher Friedrich Nietzsche was born. By 1883, 40 years after the first telegraph message was sent, Nietzsche declared the death of God. His proclamation is widely acknowledged as a harbinger of the end of modernity, a seed that would eventually blossom into the postmodern age.[4]

The graphic and electronic revolutions of the 19th century

"THE AGE OF PRINT, WHICH HELD SWAY FROM APPROXIMATELY 1500 TO 1900, HAD ITS OBITUARY TAPPED OUT BY THE TELEGRAPH, THE FIRST OF THE NEW ELECTRIC MEDIA."[1]

"TODAY WE EXPERIENCE IN REVERSE WHAT PRE-LITERATE MAN FACED WITH THE ADVENT OF WRITING."[2]

—MARSHALL MCLUHAN, 1964

created the conditions necessary for the rise of the postmodern age. In the same way the printing press gave rise to modernity, electronic media were the primary agents in bringing about postmodernity, demolishing our concentration on abstract doctrine, and changing our beliefs about truth. This correlation illustrates McLuhan's saying: "We shape our tools and afterward our tools shape us."[5]

A HALL OF MIRRORS

Now that we've spent some time exploring the cultural effects of phonetic writing and the printing press, we should be able to make quick work of assessing the impact of electronic and digital media.[6] However, the nature of these media forms makes this discussion much more precarious. The world of electronic communication is an absolute maelstrom, as McLuhan observed in the '60s, and it has gotten exponentially more complex in the subsequent 40 years.

In the communication arts building at the university I attended, there was a room legendary for its unusual design. It was a small, eight-sided room with couches arranged in a circle. The walls consisted of padded panels covered with beige felt. But this wasn't the strange part. The panels had hinges, and on the other side of each panel was a full-sized mirror. To this day I have no idea what educational function this served other than entertainment value for professors. Here's what I mean:

One day, as an "experiment," our professor flipped the panels before we arrived and transformed the room into an octagon of mirrors. As soon as we entered the room, we were confronted by a panoramic set of reflections reflecting reflections. If you've ever been in a hall of mirrors at a carnival, you know the effect—it feels like a kind of blindness. Our hands became our eyes, as though we had entered a dark room. Slowly, with outstretched arms, we felt our way to the couches. We had been in that room many times, but our ability to discern reflection from reality was almost completely obliterated by the mirror images. Even once safely seated, we were so disoriented and distracted that we had to flip the panels back in order to carry on with class.

This experience illustrates a truth of our current media environment: Electronic culture presents us with a disorienting hall of mirrors where media are embedded in other media. Nearly every new digital or electronic technology contains, retrieves, and restructures a previous medium. The telegraph retrieves and restructures electricity and the printed word. The cell phone retrieves and restructures radio and the telephone. These are just simple media hybrids, but the media relationships get more disorienting when we talk about the Internet, which contains and reflects a dozen different media forms—radio, film, television, telephones, etc. Given this complex reality, it is extremely difficult to isolate, analyze, and assess the nature of electronic media and the way they shape the church.

Bruce Lee: The Master of Mirrors

Still, it is worth the effort. To help us work through this analysis, I will be drawing from an unusual source. Obviously Bruce Lee was not a media theorist, but a legendary martial artist and movie star. In 1973 he starred in a movie called *Enter the Dragon* in which he encountered his own hall of mirrors. His experience there teaches us a lesson about navigating electronic culture.

In the movie, Lee plays a secret agent sent to infiltrate the remote island lair of Han, a corrupt heroin dealer. In the climactic final fight sequence Han lures Lee into a hall of mirrors. Lee immediately experiences the same disorienting blindness my classmates and I did. He is suddenly unable to identify or strike his opponent, who appears and disappears in multiple reflections like a ghost. Han, on the other hand, is repeatedly able to blindside Lee with a kick or a punch and then hide in the reflections again. At one point Lee zeros in on Han and performs a flying drop kick, only to shatter a mirror—foiled again. Lee fails to land that crucial blow, but the broken mirror gives him an idea. He quickly realizes that if he begins breaking mirrors, it will reduce the number of reflections, thereby destroying the illusion of his enemy. Immediately, Lee sets himself to shattering mirrors. Finally, with only a few mirrors still standing, Lee recovers his bearings, finds his foe, and defeats him to save the day.

When it comes to understanding electronic media, Lee's strategy is quite useful. We need to begin by removing as many mirrors and reflections as possible, leaving only those inventions that caused the most radical break with previous ways of communicating. Naturally, I'm not arguing for some Luddite strategy of literally destroying media. I'm suggesting the easiest way to get our bearings is to focus our attention on a few basic inventions.

It is my contention that the most significant inventions of the electronic age include the telegraph, the radio, and the photograph.

My premise is quite simple: just as the printing press amplified the power of phonetic literacy, so, too, cell phones and the Internet amplify the power of earlier media like the telegraph and radio. Therefore, the best way to understand current innovations is to study these earlier inventions. This distinction between *inventions* and *innovations* is an important one. Leonard Sweet articulates this well:

> Invention comes from the root word *inventus*, which means to start from scratch and discover something new. Innovation's root word is *nova*. Nova means to make new again, to take something that already exists and make it fresh or to put it into practice or to combine it with something else so that something happens.[7]

Therefore, we will spend our time looking at the early inventions as the interpretive keys to later innovations. Once we have isolated a few mirrors and established our bearings, we will be better prepared to start adding mirrors without losing our equilibrium.

HOW ELECTRONIC MEDIA IS SHAPING THE CHURCH

Between 1850 and 1900 the entire communication structure in America eroded under the torrent of the graphic and electronic revolutions.[8] Driven by the economic imperative of the Industrial Revolution, a slew of inventions appeared. Chief among them were the three I mentioned above: the telegraph, the radio, and the photograph. As they converged with one another in later innovations, their ability to alter the way we perceive the world equaled that of the printing press.

In the remainder of this chapter, we will see how the telegraph brought about the death of "absolute truth" and the rise of relativism, thereby undermining the notion that the Bible is an unshakable foundation of "Truth." We will see how radio reversed the individualism of print, bringing about a new tribalism in the church. Finally, we will devote most of our attention to the effects of the "Graphic Revolution"—the unprecedented production and dissemination of photography and images to the masses.[9] We will see how the flood of images in our culture is leading Western churches to adopt characteristics of the Eastern Orthodox Church, how it retrieves the medieval Catholic emphasis on communion over preaching, and how it is changing our concept of conversion from a single binary event to an ongoing process of transformation.

TELEGRAPH: THE VICTORIAN INTERNET

The invention of printing from movable type launched the greatest expansion and organization of knowledge in the history of the world. However, it was not responsible for creating the character of our current Information Age. That honor belongs to the telegraph. Morse's invention did something that dramatically altered the nature of information: it broke the connection between communication and transportation for the first time in history. Prior to the telegraph, information traveled at about 35 miles per hour—roughly the speed of a train.[10] But when information was translated into an electric pulse, it was freed from the bonds of time and space and able to travel at the speed of light. This was a spectacular breakthrough in the 19th century. However, its remarkable speed distracted people from the true marvel of the technology—its ability to alter a worldview.

Prior to the telegraph, information tended to be local, rooted in a context, and wrapped in history to provide meaning and coherence. Even encyclopedias that provided global information were laden with context and history. With the telegraph, information was instantly rent from its local and historical setting. It was presented as a mosaic of unrelated data points with no apparent connection, causes, or meaning. Prior to the telegraph, information was gathered for the purpose of deepening our understanding and wisdom. But with the telegraph, information became a commodity in itself, something that could be bought and sold. Its price was determined by how fast and how far it traveled. As Neil Postman observes, "The principal strength of the telegraph was its capacity to move information, not collect it, explain it, or analyze it."[11] As a result, information itself changed to the point where "there is no sense of proportion to be discerned in the world. Events are entirely idiosyncratic; history is irrelevant; there is no rational basis for valuing one thing over another."[12]

We see this clearly today. Consider the front page of a newspaper or news website. With the information unified only by a dateline, we are assailed by unrelated data points presented on equal footing—Scott Peterson Found Guilty…Two Marines Killed in Iraq…Britney Spears Ties the Knot…Notre Dame Football Coach Fired…Bin Laden Issues New Video—and on it goes. Our challenge becomes figuring out how to prioritize and find meaning in this plurality of disparate events that frame our window on the world.

As always, our worldview and thinking patterns mirror our media—we become what we behold. As the telegraph wrapped the world in a web of wires, it began to whisper a new subliminal message: truth itself is, in Postman's words, "entirely idiosyncratic; history is irrelevant; there is no rational basis for valuing one thing over another." Under this influence, it didn't take long for Nietzsche to adopt a nihilistic worldview and declare the death of God.

In more recent years, the telegraph has extended its embrace through other information technologies like TV, personal computers, and the Internet. These media forms have continued to till the cultural soil and nurture the rise of relativism and the death of the belief in absolute truth.

As our thinking patterns begin to mirror this communication pattern, we find it only natural to deny any sense of a *metanarrative*, an overarching story or truth that organizes and makes sense of all other truths. The notion of the metanarrative gained ascendancy during the modern era. This was due in part to the print age, which as we know gave rise to objectivity, repeatability, and uniformity. This emphasis reinforced the belief in a grand, central story that organizes and gives meaning to all other stories. This was good news for the church, because it retrieved and legitimized many of the truth claims of Scripture. But the subliminal messages of electronic media undermined this belief. The glut of disparate, often contradictory, and random data with no center or margin has begun to erode our belief in a metanarrative.

As a result, authority, truth, and meaning become difficult to discover and establish with clarity or certainty. Doubts trickle in, and we find the notion of a single grand story that unifies everything to be absurd and even arrogant. In this sense, the telegraph tapped out the obituary of the metanarrative. The death of the metanarrative has become a defining characteristic of postmodernity.[13] It hasn't taken long for people in current cultures to see the truth claims of Scripture as no more valid than the claims of Dr. Phil.

This aspect of postmodernity is quite possibly the greatest challenge to the claims of Christ. Nothing could be more inconsistent with Scripture than to suggest that there is no such thing as a metanarrative. The Bible clearly proclaims a metanarrative, the grand story of God reconciling the world to himself in Christ. This challenge makes understanding the role of media in bringing about the death of the metanarrative much more than an intellectual exercise. It is a crucial calling of the church in the postmodern age.

CHANGING METAPHORS FOR HOW WE KNOW WHAT WE KNOW

Given the cultural influence of philosophy, it is worth considering how emerging technology shaped this field of study. A major shift from the philosophy of modernism to postmodernism occurred in an area known as *epistemology*. This word simply refers to the study of how we develop knowledge or how we know what we know. In her book *Anglo-American Postmodernity*, Nancey Murphy explains that the shift can be most clearly seen in the metaphors used by the modern and postmodern camps.[14] In the modern era, philosophers used the metaphor of a building to describe knowledge—there is a foundation of basic belief upon which all other knowledge rests. In more recent years, postmodern philosophers have employed the metaphor of a web to describe epistemology—beliefs are connected to one another in myriad ways.[15] However, no one has observed the simple fact that these changes in our metaphors are a direct result of changes in our forms of media. The diagram below (Figure 6) describes the differences between these metaphors and illustrates the media connection.

MODERN METAPHOR Derived from Print	POSTMODERN METAPHOR Derived from Telegraph
PRACTICE THEOLOGY SCRIPTURE	
KNOWLEDGE AS BUILDING	*KNOWLEDGE AS WEB*
The modern approach to knowledge, known as *foundationalism*, was conceived during the Enlightenment. In this understanding all truth is derived from a single foundation. Knowledge is then added on top of this foundation. Knowledge builds in one direction, from the foundation to the top floor. It is a one-way, linear, sequential metaphor in which the foundation determines everything above it. Notice the way this directly mirrors the one-way, line-by-line, letter-by-letter form of the printed page.	The postmodern approach to knowledge, known as the *web of belief*, was developed by Willard V. Quine in 1970. In this conception, knowledge is conditioned both by our experience and by truth claims. These truth claims have multiple interconnections with each other. They form a web bound by, but not rooted in, experience. There is no foundation; instead the legitimacy of a web is determined by its coherence. More interconnections mean a more coherent belief system. It is a two-way dialogue in which experience shapes belief and belief shapes experience. Notice the way in which this metaphor directly mirrors the web of interconnections and dialogue that comprise the telegraph and other information technologies.

FIGURE 6

This shift in philosophical thinking is not simply an abstract idea. It is expressed in the day-to-day assumptions of modern and postmodern cultures as well. I once had an interesting conversation with a coworker in advertising. John and I had gone to lunch many times, but on this day the conversation turned to religion. I was excited because I considered myself a missionary in the secular corporate world. It turned out John had heard the gospel message many times but had never found it compelling. I saw my mission field and went forth.

At one point in the conversation John said, "I don't get it. Why do I need to believe in Jesus to go to heaven?" I offered what I understood as the most succinct answer to this question: "Well, there is a huge gap between us and God because of our sin, and so God sent Jesus to bridge that gap for us." Having established this, I prepared for the typical follow-up question like, "But how did Jesus accomplish this?" The question never came. Instead John responded by saying, "I don't think there is any gap between me and God, so I guess I don't need Jesus." I was tripped up by this but moved on undeterred. I informed John that the Bible tells us that there *is* a gap between us and God. He cordially responded, "I realize that, but the Bible is *your* authority. Don't get me wrong; I think that's cool. It's just not my authority." It didn't take long before we moved on to another topic of conversation.

For days after, I replayed that conversation in my head, wondering what else I could have said that would have been more compelling. It wasn't until I learned the difference between modern and postmodern epistemologies that I realized something. Although neither of us could have articulated it at the time, we were operating from two different assumptions about knowledge. I was basing everything on my modernist assumption that Scripture is the foundation of truth. He was operating out of a postmodern assumption in which the interplay of his experiences and popular ideologies formed a web that seemed cogent to him. In one sense, I wasn't trying to convert him to Christ; I was trying to convert him to a modern worldview—a futile exercise for those of you who haven't tried it. This is an important distinction, because once we understand it, the nature of evangelism changes entirely, and we are no longer bound to outmoded methods of apologetics. Instead we are free to experiment and try new ways of communicating the message of the gospel and inviting people into the life of faith.

RADIO: THE TRIBAL DRUM BEATS AGAIN

A second 19th-century invention had an equally powerful, albeit different, effect on culture. The medium of radio returned us once again to the tribal campfire where the resonant echoes of the spoken word and corporate experiences began to reshape our thinking. McLuhan was among the first to recognize that electronic media were leading to the retribalization of our culture. He observed, "Radio provided the first massive experience of electronic implosion, that reversal of the entire direction and meaning of literate Western civilization."[16]

With radio, we began to share simultaneous oral experiences on a scale never before known to human culture. This simultaneous occurrence of a fleeting oral/aural event was a radical reversal of the fragmentation and individualization brought on in the print age: a book is consumed on one's own private time, but to participate in the radio event, everyone must huddle around the radio receiver at the same moment and listen. Just as in tribal cultures, the radio, allows shared songs, experiences, and stories to emerge, but with radio, these extend far beyond the perimeter of the local campfire.

Radio also retrieves the surround-sound world of acoustic space for the masses. As we know, the move from oral tradition to the printed word had profound implications for humanity. The visual sense is highly controlled, detached, and always maintains a specific point of view with a focus and a periphery.[17] When I look at my computer screen, I see it from only one point of view—mine. All I have to do is look in another direction, and the screen is either in my peripheral vision or has totally disappeared. Sight, therefore, is a highly controllable and detached sense.

In contrast, oral communication occurs in acoustic space. This is an all at once, surround-sound world in which there is no center or margin and where all utterance is invasive and fleeting. As I write this, I can hear people splashing in a pool, a baby crying, and someone playing guitar. Sound fills the air, not parts of the air. All of these stimuli invade my ears to varying degrees. I have some internal ability to focus on one sound more than another, but I cannot simply turn my ear in another direction to block it out completely, as I can with my eyes. Nor do we have "ear lids" that allow us to shut out sound. The ear immerses us in a resonant world of acoustic space. Radio snaps us back to tribal ways of knowing that are experiential, oral, and corporate rather than rational, visual, and private.

This shift from private to corporate ways of knowing has provided a positive corrective to the print age bias toward individualism. Within Christianity, we are moving from modernity's focus on an individualistic gospel to more communal understandings in which the message of Jesus is directed at us, not just *me*. However, before we celebrate our new emphasis on community, we should recognize that radio did not initiate a return to a purely oral culture. We are still a culture that is largely dependent upon literacy. In this sense, our culture is neither tribal nor individual. Instead, we are a paradoxical hybrid—a tribe of individuals. It is a phenomenon in which we are pulled in opposite directions and deal with new strains, tensions, and traumas for which we are quite unprepared. The impact of this phenomenon on forming community and becoming the church is immense and will be explored more fully in Chapter Six.

THE GRAPHIC REVOLUTION: DERAILING MODERNITY

The Graphic Revolution of the 19th century began when the photograph converged with the rotary press and the telegraph, allowing icons and images to be mass-produced and sent everywhere at once. The power and scope of this revolution is so significant that it demands we devote more time to its effects than we did to the telegraph and radio.

In many ways the Graphic Revolution returned us to the iconic world of the Middle Ages, only the images were recast at the speed of light and invaded our vision from every direction. Over time this iconic symbol system has been dissolving our dependence upon literacy. Corporate logos are the most obvious example of this phenomenon. There are hundreds of corporate icons that no longer require any phonetic descriptor for them to be recognizable. Icons such as McDonald's golden arches, the Target bull's-eye, Apple's apple with a bite, and the Playboy bunny no longer need words for people to identify their meaning.

The rise of image-based communication in our culture weakened our preference for abstract and linear thought patterns in favor of more concrete, holistic, and nonlinear approaches to the world. The establishment of black-and-white categories resulting from typography gave way to a preference for grayscale gradations of mystery and ambiguity that resulted from communication through images.

Regardless of what is being depicted in a photograph, the form itself evokes in us a particular pattern of intuitive, holistic thinking and emotion—the exact opposite of the patterns evoked by the printed word. We have all heard the cliché "A picture is worth a thousand words." Implied in this sentiment is the idea that images communicate information more efficiently than words. In some cases this is true, but the saying misses a greater truth. It assumes that one medium can function interchangeably with the other; thus, they are often put in competing positions. But in reality neither medium can accomplish what the other can. They are fundamentally different modes of discourse that create fundamentally different outcomes.

It would be impossible for me to communicate the ideas contained in this book using only images—the form prohibits the content. At the same time, many aspects of our faith and life, such as profound grief or joy, are beyond words and are only given utterance through the imagery of painting, photography, or even dance.[18]

To see how this is true, consider the impact of the content below.

The boy is sad.

What effect does this have on you? For most of us it is just a statement that conveys an idea—there is no real impact. Now turn the page to consider the same content in a different medium.

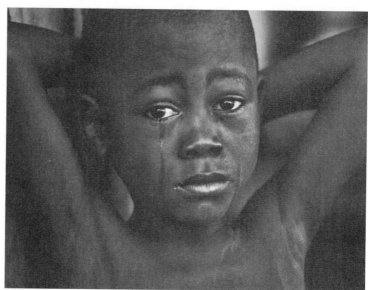

©1995, The Washington Post. Photo by Carol Guzy.

How does this image affect you? For most people it strikes in the gut, evoking a similar sadness. The basic content of the image is the same as that conveyed in the phonetic description, but because of the form, it has a radically different impact.

To understand why this is true, the diagram below (Figure 7) compares the printed word to the graphic image. They are different in three primary ways: the form of the medium, the way they are processed by the brain, and the content they are best suited to convey.

The boy
is sad.

	PRINTED WORD	IMAGE
FORM	Propositional & sequential	Presentational & holistic
PROCESS	Rational & linear (left brain)	Intuitive & nonlinear (right brain)
CONTENT	Abstraction about experience	Concrete representations of experience

FIGURE 7

The image has a powerful ability to evoke strong empathy or sadness; it is a visceral and intuitive response. In contrast, the printed statement is an abstract proposition about an experience rather than a concrete presentation of an experience.[19] Our brain processes each of these in very different ways. The printed word is processed primarily in the left hemisphere of the brain, which specializes in logic, sequence, and categories. In contrast, photographs and other imagery are processed primarily in the right hemisphere, which specializes in intuition and perceiving the *gestalt*—or everything at once.[20]

In some ways we could replace the headings "Printed Word" and "Image" in Figure 7 above with "Modernity" and "Postmodernity" respectively. It is an oversimplification, but it hints at important distinctions between the two worldviews. In this sense, the right-brained, nonlinear, and experiential nature of images gave rise to these same emphases in postmodernity. Under the torrent of images in our culture, we have seen the left-brain bias of the print age and modernity beginning to dissolve.

As image-based communication becomes the dominant symbol system in our culture, it not only changes the way we think but also determines what we think about. Images are not well-suited to articulate arguments, categories, or abstractions. They are far better suited for presenting impressions and concrete realities. Thanks to TV, political discourse in America is now based on intuition rather than reason. A presidential candidate is more likely to be elected if he appears likable, attractive, and trustworthy, all of which are subjective, intuitive evaluations based not on careful, left-brained analysis of a candidate's policy positions but on the right-brain impression of the mosaic television images.

THE WEST MOVES EAST

Because it is dependent on right-brain thinking, image-based communication actually reduces our capacity for abstract and critical reasoning skills, regardless of what is conveyed. As iconic communication has caused our thinking to become more concrete and intuitive, Western culture has embraced elements of Eastern thought patterns. Cultural commentator and publisher of metaphilm.com Read Mercer Schuchardt has observed that even the phonetic alphabet—the very thing that once differentiated the West from the East—has been co-opted by the Graphic Revolution. Schuchardt has created what he calls the brand alphabet, in which he identifies a corporate logo for every letter of the alphabet. This may seem like an odd bit of trivia until you recall that the phonetic alphabet is a system whose effectiveness depends entirely on meaningless symbols. With the brand alphabet, these symbols are given meaning for the first time. As a result, they function like ideographic symbols rather than phonetic ones. The impact on our culture is profound as the Western world begins to adopt Eastern approaches to the world (see Figure 8).

SYMBOL	夫	L	
MEANING	Strong Man	Nothing	Lexus Luxury Car
ATTRIBUTES	Holistic Concrete	Fragmented, Abstract	Holistic, Concrete

FIGURE 8

The subtle adoption of Eastern values has had a significant influence in shaping Western postmodern culture. In many ways, postmodernity has more in common with Eastern modes of thought than the distinctly modern ones of the West.

As images become major elements of the culture, critical reasoning gives way to a preference for the experiential and intuitive. For the church, the result is a new appreciation for Eastern Orthodox practices and a retrieval of the medieval Catholic Church.[21] Much of Eastern Orthodox theology is wrapped around the use of images and icons as a part of worship, and the Eastern Orthodox practice of contemplating icons is gaining popularity as a spiritual discipline in the West.[22] Moreover, emerging churches are intentionally designing worship services that engage all five senses.[23] This emphasis on multisensory worship is borrowed heavily from the Eastern Orthodox tradition in which theological significance is assigned to body movement, incense, chanting, bells, eating, and images.

As Eastern Orthodox practices are increasingly incorporated by the emerging church, our theology begins to reflect the Eastern preference for mystery and experience rather than reason and evidence.

If we become what we behold, it is no surprise that Orthodox worship demonstrates a preference for sacred mystery over systematic theology and intuitive sensory experience over critical reasoning. These preferences reflect the biases of image-based thinking. There are very few "systematic theologians" in the Eastern Orthodox tradition. The reason is that systematic theology (a product of the print age) seeks to explain and categorize, while images can only provide impressions and intuitions. In this sense, the pursuit of explanation and understanding runs counter to the bias of icons and images.

Not only are we incorporating the Eastern Church with this new iconic world, but we are also retrieving elements of the medieval Catholic Church. With the rise of images in culture, we are seeing a retrieval of medieval church symbols. Many churches in the West are beginning to employ digitized reproductions of medieval stained glass windows and projecting them onto screens as a part of worship. It is not uncommon to hear arguments for using images in worship that sound something like this: "Emerging generations are increasingly formed by image-based media like TV, film, and the Internet. That means we need to adopt these cultural expressions for worship to be relevant." However, our adoption of images in worship is not merely an imitative practice; it is also generative. We now know that the use of images changes the way we perceive everything, including the gospel.

Moving beyond this literal retrieval of medieval symbols, churches are recovering medieval Catholic practices as well. The eucharistic meal is once again growing in importance; in some churches it has displaced the sermon entirely as the centerpiece of worship. A number of emerging church worship services I have visited involve little more than a meal and music—there is no sermon at all.

The preference for this mystical and experiential ritual owes much to the shaping effects of the Graphic Revolution. I believe these are primarily positive changes as they reconnect us to aspects of the faith that have long been suppressed under the left-brain tyranny of the print age. In many ways I believe God is at work in our media revolution, correcting the cultural extremes that resulted from overextended technologies.

At the same time, there may be unintended consequences of our efforts to utilize images. We may be in danger of undoing some of the most valuable aspects of modernity's influence on Christian faith, such as our dependence on the medium of Scripture or the development of leaders who are well-versed in our sacred texts. We need to be intentional and deliberate about how we use imagery, being careful not to supplant the tyranny of the left brain with the tyranny of the right brain. Like the brain itself, we must strive to hold these two distinct and opposing ways of thinking in equilibrium.

REDISCOVERING THE PARABLES AND THE DISAPPEARANCE OF PAUL

Clearly, this preference for concrete images rather than abstract propositions can be a great gift to the church. This movement has restored our right-brain preference for metaphor, poetry, and story—the linguistic version of images. Because of this, we have grown in our appreciation for the synoptic Gospels (Matthew, Mark, and Luke) and the parables of Jesus, which actually went out of fashion to some degree during the print age. At the same time, this appreciation can lead to a waning interest in the writings of Paul, an imbalance that was prevalent prior to the Reformation, an imbalance Martin Luther worked hard to remedy.

It might surprise some to learn that in his preface to the New Testament, Luther offered an evaluation of the New Testament Canon. In a section called "Which Are the True and Noblest Books of the New Testament?" Luther writes, "John's gospel is the one, fine, true, and chief gospel, and is far, far to be preferred over the other three and placed high above them. So, too, the epistles of St. Paul and St. Peter far surpass the other three gospels, Matthew, Mark, and Luke."[24] Luther's reasoning was simple—anything in Scripture that tells the *story of* Jesus was far less helpful than books describing explicit *doctrines about* Jesus.

It should not be surprising that Luther, who was shaped by the technology of print, would venerate the more abstract and literate treatises in Scripture. The Gospel of John and Paul's writings, while certainly containing story and metaphor, are primarily characterized by highly theological, abstract, and lengthy propositional discourses, whereas the synoptic Gospels are characterized by short, rhythmic blocks of concrete stories and parables rooted in the thought patterns of an oral tradition. Luther observed that John's gospel provides us with more of Jesus' abstract teaching and theology while Matthew, Mark, and Luke provide us with Jesus' concrete life and miracles.

Paul's writings are comprised of both concrete metaphors

and abstract theology. In this way, they represent a complex interplay of a literate mind in an oral culture. However, Paul's extensive use of rational syllogisms (i.e., if/then patterns) and abstract propositions are the main reason the Reformation and modernity could retrieve and overextend him so easily. This literate character, which permeates his writings, is also the reason he is at risk of disappearing in our electronic age.

Images are simply not well-suited to convey his abstract, rational prose. As I mentioned earlier, you won't see concepts such as "For in the gospel a righteousness from God is revealed, a righteousness that is by faith from first to last" (Romans 1:17) depicted as an image in a stained glass window—the explicit and multilayered meaning would be completely lost. In this sense, if we fail to understand how images shape both our cognitive capacities and our message, we might soon find ourselves replicating the medieval tendency to de-emphasize Paul.

CONVERSION IN THE ELECTRONIC ERA

The modern church's renewed interest in Paul was certainly good for the church. Additionally, it led to some interesting theological shifts, particularly in the way the church thought about conversion. In the modern age, there was a great deal of emphasis on conversion as an event. The moment you repented for your sins and believed in Jesus, your name got moved from the "unsaved" column in God's accounting ledger to the "saved" column—you were officially converted. Paul articulates this in Romans 10:9: "If you confess with your mouth, 'Jesus is Lord,' and believe in your heart that God raised him from the dead, you will be saved."

It's hard to argue with Paul. However, in the postmodern age, we have begun to discover that Scripture isn't unified on this issue. For example, we might ask when the disciples moved from the unsaved column to the saved column. Before the Resurrection, what would they have believed themselves to be saved from? The confession of Peter is certainly a significant event, but there is no indication that this is the moment he got saved. Instead, the Gospel writers show us that the disciples had an unfolding experience of discovery and growth. Their conversion was not a binary event so much as a gradual process. In the postmodern age, thanks in part to the dominance of images, there has been an increasing acceptance of a process conception of conversion.[25]

This is again due to the changes brought on by the rise of image-based communication. As already noted, images depict concrete realities, whereas written language is able to create abstract categories. For example, we use written or spoken language to create categories like "apples" and "oranges." These categories don't really exist; we invented these labels to give meaning and order to our world. This is one reason God told Adam to name the animals in the garden—it brought order out of chaos and classification to an infinite variety of creatures. The medium of print profoundly intensifies this kind of thinking, so much so that during the age of printing, our culture became nearly obsessed with classification, categories, and explanation.

As images displace the written word for communication, our thinking patterns and preferences change. A photograph cannot create categories; it just provides an impression of reality. An image shows us the world as it is—an array of ambiguity and mystery. It does not explain or organize the world the way language can. As a result, we become increasingly tolerant of ambiguity and mystery—the very things images can best depict.[26] As printing wanes, so also does our preoccupation with creating categories.

Because images are fast becoming the dominant symbol system by which our culture makes meaning, the emerging church is less likely to view conversion in binary terms. The strict cognitive categories of "believer" and "nonbeliever," "saved" and "unsaved," "the elect" and "the nonelect" were intensified and codified during the age of print. But in an electronic age conditioned by images, we have begun to believe that categories oversimplify the complex mystery of God's relationship to God's people and the dynamic reality of a life of faith.

Evidence of this shift can be seen in the metaphors we use to describe evangelism. The images of courtroom dramas, warriors, and crusades are diminishing. These metaphors emphasize clearly opposing categories of good and evil, right and wrong, saved and unsaved. The new metaphors for evangelism come from the worlds of gardening, dialogue, and dancing. These images emphasize the mystery of process, the continual ebb and flow of two or more people seeking truth together in an ongoing state of humble discovery. The moment when a person is moved from the unsaved category to the saved category is less important than the unfolding of this process.

For nearly every Christian, faith lives somewhere between trusting and doubt. Its intensity and color are shaped by seasons of grief and hope, passion and despair. In this way, static categories for evangelism and discipleship become increasingly elusive and difficult to maintain. In an emerging context, it is assumed that both Christians and non-Christians are in need of ongoing conversion experiences. We are called to a continual process of redemption, reconciliation, and daily conforming to the likeness of Christ. The categories of believer and nonbeliever still have significance, but they are beginning to serve a different purpose. They are no longer used to define a target for evangelism. Rather, these categories inform the starting point and tone of our conversations with one another.

While this shift is generally a positive one, we cannot deny the repeated examples in Scripture where conversion is depicted as a dramatic event. Paul's Damascus experience is a quintessential example of such a conversion. These dramatic events are important and should be marked or ritualized. For some people, conversion will be a dramatic event. I certainly had a clear moment that marks the day I became a Christian. But there is room for both the dramatic event and the recognition that even such an event is only the beginning of living in the way of Jesus. In the end, the process approach to conversion opens us to more ways of seeing God's work in God's people. In this way, the process view should supplement, not displace, the event view of conversion.

BOTH EYES OPEN: RESTORING DEPTH PERCEPTION FOR THE PATH AHEAD

Like yeast slowly permeating dough, the full impact of the electronic age did not become discernible on a mass scale until the mid-to late 20th century. The growth of this worldview was accelerated exponentially when the effects of the telegraph, radio, and photograph converged into television. The power of television was then extended by the rise of visually interactive media such as the Internet. The church in the 21st century is now confronting the challenges outlined above on a scale exponentially greater than in the 19th century.

In an effort to codify and summarize these discoveries, we turn once more to McLuhan's four laws. Instead of considering every electronic medium on its own, we will consider the four questions in relation to electronic culture as a whole. Once again, there is no definitive set of answers to these questions. The ones I offer below are only my own impressions; there are many other observations to be made.

THE EFFECTS OF ELECTRONIC CULTURE

Electronic culture intensifies a right brain encounter with God, corporate approaches to faith, and our reliance on intuition and experience for knowing God.

When electronic culture is taken to an extreme, it reverses into relativism. It also reverses our capacity for abstract thought and critical reasoning skills.

ENHANCES

RETRIEVES

REVERSES INTO

OBOLESCES

Electronic culture retrieves Eastern Orthodox and medieval Catholic spirituality (i.e., contemplating icons). It also retrieves the gospel's story of Jesus as central to faith.

Electronic culture obsolesces our belief in the metanarrative. It obsolesces our belief that conversion is a one-time, binary event. Finally, it obsolesces the role of abstract propositional faith and the full impact of Paul's letters.

FIGURE 9

This chapter concludes Part I of the book—"New Ways to Perceive." We have developed the two-eyed vision necessary for perceiving the power of media and technology. We have discovered that media forms, regardless of their content, have a profound and subliminal power to shape the way we think. We have learned to ask different questions of our media as a way of anticipating their unintended consequences. We have seen the ways in which the printing press was a primary force in shaping the modern evangelical church. We have seen how the communications revolution of the 19th century planted seeds that are now breaking through the topsoil in the form of the emerging church.

I want to reiterate an important point. These are not the only causes of such shifts in the church or culture—rather, they are the ones most overlooked. Our goal all along has been to develop a kind of radar for perceiving the true nature and power of media and technology to shape the way we think and interact. Armed with this radar, we are better equipped to detect and engage the unique challenges and opportunities of electronic culture with discernment, authenticity, and faithfulness to the gospel. In Part II of this book we will work to apply this perspective to specific church practices and reimagine the way they might look in the postmodern age.

PART II: ALTERNATIVE WAYS TO PRACTICE

In the second part of this book, we will follow McLuhan's advice and stand back to perceive the entire whirling maelstrom of electronic culture as a whole. Instead of looking at individual media, we will consider the whole of electronic culture. Having regained some equilibrium, we can reenter the hall of mirrors, but this time with new vision. Having trained our eyes to see the power of media, we are now able to turn our attention more fully to considering its implications for our faith.

Our exploration will begin with a discussion of the essence of God's chosen medium—the church (Chapter Five). After developing a shared understanding of what it means to be the people of God, we will consider how the church can respond to the challenges and opportunities of electronic and emerging culture. Specifically, we will look at the ways we form community (Chapter Six); the challenges of power, authority, and leadership (Chapter Seven); and the force and form of emerging worship in the electronic age (Chapter Eight).

Noticeably absent are chapters related to evangelism or mission. The reason for this is simple. All three of the practices above are missional in nature; they are some of the most important "media" that communicate our message. The way we form and interact in community, the way we understand leadership, and the way we worship are all missional activities that shape and reveal God's message before a watching world. In other words, the way we live and practice our faith together is an evangelistic, missional activity that communicates our distinct identity. Our identity is the message.

Finally, in the chapters that follow I offer some concrete recommendations for how we might alter these practices to reflect and convey God's message more faithfully. All of these recommendations should be held with an open hand and assessed in your own cultural and theological contexts. They are not intended as prescriptions but rather as catalysts for further conversation and creativity.

EVOLVING THE MEDIUM AND THE MESSAGE

CHAPTER FIVE

When I first read McLuhan, I found it disconcerting to discover the subliminal power of media to shape my view of the world. I wasn't fond of the thought that I might be unknowingly controlled or manipulated by the media forms involved in nearly every aspect of my life. I didn't like the idea that I was a fish oblivious to the hook holding the worm. Why didn't anybody ever warn me about this?

"MEDIA ARE 'MAKE HAPPEN' AGENTS, NOT 'MAKE AWARE' AGENTS."[1]

"THERE IS ABSOLUTELY NO INEVITABILITY AS LONG AS THERE IS A WILLINGNESS TO CONTEMPLATE WHAT IS HAPPENING."[2]

—MARSHALL MCLUHAN

This was so troubling that I began looking at McLuhan's critics, only to find few who offered compelling critiques. The more I studied and explored, the more I resigned myself to agreeing that McLuhan was right and that media have the power to change us, whether we know it or not. I remember thinking, *If media inevitably shape us this much, what are we supposed to do? How are we supposed to respond?* This felt a bit like trying to stop the wind and the tides.

Over the years I have searched for answers to these questions. While there was no single lightning bolt to clarify everything, eventually an inkling of an answer began to emerge. It seemed too simple to be useful at first and felt like a cop-out. However, the more I lived with it, the more I became convinced it offered a legitimate direction for my understanding. It will not surprise you that the answer initially came from one of McLuhan's many sayings: "There is absolutely no inevitability as long as there is a willingness to contemplate what is happening."[3] In other words, the hidden effects of media are not inevitable when we seek to understand the things that shape us. Too often we want to determine whether something is good or bad before we understand it. But doing so means we will always encounter our media with the flat-footed enthusiasm of Mr. No Depth Perception.

The awareness we've gained through our examination of media thus far is perhaps the most critical faculty necessary to develop navigational skills for dealing with the hidden and formative powers of our media and technology. Just by becoming aware that the medium shapes both the message and ourselves, we are well on our way to responding appropriately. However, this awareness means we need to revisit the evangelical rallying cry: "The methods change, but the message stays the same."

THE EVER-CHANGING MESSAGE

Obviously, our methods for communicating God's message have undergone a series of seismic shifts. Because the medium is the message, our media revolutions—from the printing press to the Internet—have led to unintended changes in our message. Among them is a shift from a modern, individualistic, and highly rational concept of the gospel to a postmodern, communal, holistic, and experiential one. These innovations are not occurring in a vacuum. They are partly the result of reading Scripture through the new interpretive lenses created by our media.

Like it or not, our theology and interpretation of Scripture have a long history of mirroring our forms of media, a fact most easily seen in the way modern approaches to faith mirror the linear, rational, and abstract attributes of the printed word. This is not an inherently negative reality, especially if we're aware that it's happening. In fact, I believe some of our methods, and thus our message, *should* change and evolve—this is part of God's ongoing creation and relationship to God's people.

The church needn't fear such change. Long before Marshall McLuhan made his observation that the medium is the message, Jesus expressed this same intimate connection. We find an important object lesson concerning Jesus' methods and message in the Gospel of Matthew:

> No one sews a piece of unshrunk cloth on an old cloak, for the patch pulls away from the cloak, and a worse tear is made. Neither is new wine put into old wineskins; otherwise, the skins burst, and the wine is spilled, and the skins are destroyed; but new wine is put into fresh wineskins, and so both are preserved. (Matthew 9:16-17, NRSV)

Jesus understood the intimate connection between the medium and message, the container and the content. He tells us a new container (wineskin) must bear with it new content (wine); so also old methods (worn garments) will retain an old message (worn patch). We evangelicals have long believed that the wineskins (our methods and media) must be constantly renewed and updated. But we may have missed the most dramatic point of this passage: The emphasis for Jesus is that the *wine* itself is new. Jesus came proclaiming a new message, not just new methods.

Throughout Scripture the message changes. God's message of promise to Abraham was not the same as God's message of judgment and exile for a disobedient Israel. Jesus' local, covert, and exclusive mission to the Jews as described in the Gospels was not the same as Paul's overt and universal message to the Gentiles. These messages are not inconsistent or irreconcilable. On the contrary, they are integral parts of an unfolding divine drama. Ours is the dynamic story of God and God's people at work in the world, not a set of static propositions. The gospel message is not an abstract, fixed idea but rather an unfolding, incarnational drama in which God is working to bring the world back into a reconciled relationship with himself.

Just as in Scripture, this amazing story continues to develop today in each new time and place. With each turn in the story of humanity, we are introduced to new emphases as well as potential limits on our understanding of the gospel. As we have seen, the print age led to a reductionist articulation of the gospel, first championed by the American revivalism of the 19th century, that made faith as easy as 1, 2, 3: (1) Believe in Jesus; (2) apologize for your sins; (3) go to heaven. But it also introduced us to the importance of a personal relationship with Jesus. Its heavily intellectual emphasis helped unlock the treasure chest of Paul's rich, rational, and nuanced theology that presents us with propositions, not just stories.

The emerging gospel of the electronic age is moving beyond cognitive propositions and linear formulas to embrace the power and truth of story. It revives the importance of following Jesus holistically rather than simply knowing Jesus cognitively. It has reintroduced us to a corporate understanding of faith that has powerful implications for this life, not just the next. It recovers the importance of ancient imagery, rites, and rituals in celebrating the mystery of the kingdom of God. However, it may be at risk of losing the power and grandeur of Paul's ideas and contributions and the very real propositional truth claims of Scripture.

We can also see the ways in which the message can and does change when we consider the profound differences in the gospel as it is expressed in different parts of the world. In Latin America, the gospel of Christ is understood largely as the promise of liberation from sociopolitical oppression. In this view, the ministry of Jesus and the message of God's kingdom correspond to the Exodus event in which God freed the Israelites from slavery. This is in contrast to the North American view, in which the gospel is understood primarily as forgiveness of personal sin and the promise of eternal life.

Each of these views reflects a distinctly different message. They are intimately related to the particular social context out of which they emerge. In a wealthy suburb of North America, the promise of liberation from political oppression has little meaning. In the same way, the assurance that one's personal sins are forgiven hardly provides comfort and hope amid the life-threatening oppression of corrupt dictatorships in Latin America. While both understandings represent aspects of the gospel, they are very different messages.

When we claim the gospel message is unchanging, we risk boasting of a kind of omniscience in which we presume to know the totality of God's inexhaustible mysteries. We presume to have discovered the one simple and unchanging message for all times and places. In this view, the Holy Spirit, who was sent to teach us truth, becomes little more than a dashboard ornament, for we already know all the truth we need. In this view, the gospel story (if there is one) is of no consequence; all that matters is a static proposition.

Instead of presuming to know the unchanging, universal gospel message, our posture toward the gospel should be one of humility and discovery. Throughout Scripture God invites us to remain open to the dynamic and unpredictable breath of the Holy Spirit as we seek to be God's people. Remaining faithful to Scripture does not mean holding on to some fixed and permanent idea of right doctrine until our knuckles turn white. Faithfulness means developing a communal sense of patience to discover the gospel, courage to name it, and humility to hold it with an open hand in order to allow it to be touched by God's voice in Scripture and the Spirit's movement in our midst.

I am not suggesting we can never know the gospel message or that any previous conception of the gospel is null and void. Nor am I proposing that we should have free rein to make the gospel what we want it to be without border or boundary. Such an approach would render it meaningless. Instead, I am echoing Paul's sentiment: "For now we see in a mirror dimly...Now I know only in part..." (1 Corinthians 13:12, NRSV). We must have the freedom to allow both our methods and our message to change as we continue to discover God's voice in each new context. We must accept the mystery and wonder of God's grace, which allows us to try new ways of being the church, occasionally fail, repent when necessary, and try again.

GOD'S CHOSEN MEDIUM

We have spent most of this book talking about media as extensions of humanity. But to truly understand the impact of media on the church, we need to recognize the media forms God uses to grow and change God's people.

Years ago I was talking with an acquaintance about his views on Christianity. It quickly became clear he was quite hostile to the faith, in part because he had had some negative experiences with Christians. He shared several stories of terrible hypocrisy and arrogance in the lives of some believers. Needless to say, this was a significant turnoff for him. Even worse, I knew I had been one of those believers more than once in my life. In my evangelistic anxiety, I responded to his grievances with something like, "If you want to know what Christianity is really about, don't look at Christians. They're messed up like everybody else. Instead, you should look to the Bible and Jesus." It was a noble effort to try to rescue Jesus and the gospel by severing their ties with the church. Unfortunately, it was a misguided effort, for as the church we are the body of Christ, God's chosen medium sent to be (not just to proclaim) a message of healing and hope to the world.

God's message and revelation has unfolded throughout history and will continue to evolve in each new context. The same can be said about God's choice of media. Throughout history God has used various methods to communicate the message—a spoken word, a burning bush, chiseled words on stone tablets, angels, prophets, even a donkey. Each of these media forms carries with it a different force, and each conveys a slightly different message. But the greatest medium of God's revelation to the world is Jesus Christ.

In Christ, God's medium and message are perfectly united.[4] As the opening of John's Gospel tells us, "The Word became flesh and made his dwelling among us" (1:14). More than just the words he said, the life Jesus lived was the revealed Word of God. After Jesus died and ascended into heaven, God found a way to ensure the divine presence would remain active on earth, creating the mysterious medium of the church—the body of Christ.

If God's chosen medium was Christ, and the church is the body of Christ, then the church is God's chosen medium for God's ongoing revelation to the world; the church exists to embody and proclaim the good news of God's kingdom. If the medium is the message, the message of the gospel is profoundly shaped by the way the church lives in the world.

We are the message—in all our hypocrisy and injustice, in all our giftedness and hope, in all our brokenness and bitterness, in all our faith and love. This is one of the great mysteries of God: why would God choose such a frail and inconsistent medium to embody God's abiding message? Perhaps God's message of redemption and reconciliation is carried by bent and bruised hearts to show God's stunning power to reach through human failure, sin, and sadness to bring about new life.

As has often happened in my life, I wish I could go back in time and have that conversation with my friend again. I would want to respond to his grievances about hypocritical Christians by saying, "That sounds horrible. I can see why you find Christianity so off-putting. It makes me even sadder to think that I, too, have been one of those hypocrites. I'm sorry you had to experience that." Instead, my attempt to defend the gospel only served to intensify his antagonism. I believe it would have been infinitely more valuable if I had just lamented with him and acknowledged the legitimacy of his frustration—at least as a starting point. Only then would I have had the right to invite him gently into a better hope.

Whatever God's reasons for choosing us to be the message, we should not confuse this idea with a call to perfection. Our goal as the church is not perfection. Such a goal only breeds greater hypocrisy and broadens our blind spots. Instead, we might seek by God's grace to become communities of humility, repentance, and authentic hope.

Humility comes when we see ourselves as beggars who have been gifted with food and invited to bring that food to others. Repentance demands the courage to admit our weaknesses, acknowledge our wounding of others, and seek reconciliation. Authenticity means that we bring our grievances with an honesty of emotion and openness to correction. Hope means that in spite of the relentless terrors, tragedies, and traumas of life, we abide with a stubborn confidence that there is a greater story at work—a story that does not deny these painful realities but interprets them in light of the story's ending, an ending where weeping turns to laughter, and despair dissolves into joy. These corporate virtues and practices articulate the very color and texture of the gospel story. By living them out, we are the message.

UNCOVERING THE NATURE OF GOD'S MEDIUM

The concept of the church as the message leads us to consider what exactly we mean by "the church." On the surface this is an easy question to answer, but in truth the church is a complex, dynamic, and elusive creation of God. In fact, the nature of the church is never directly described in Scripture; instead it is described indirectly through image and metaphor.

Fortunately, the electronic and graphic revolutions have renewed our cultural appreciation and preference for image and metaphor. Metaphors can make complicated ideas simpler by grounding abstract concepts in concrete and tangible realities. The abstract notion of God can be made more understandable when we view God as a father. At the same time, metaphors are open-ended and ambiguous. It is not clear exactly what attributes of a father should be applied to God—we have some idea, but the boundaries are deliberately vague.

The strength of metaphors is in their ability to anchor and explain ideas without defining hard or rigid boundaries. They are like blades of grass, able to sway with the wind while remaining rooted in one place. In this way, metaphor is an ideal way to describe something as mysterious and fluid as the church.

The New Testament offers dozens of metaphors to describe the church, frequently by identifying it in relationship to something else, such as God, God's kingdom, Jesus Christ, or the world. It is worth our time to explore a few of these metaphors before we plunge into the discussion of specific practices of the church.

The people of God

The most dominant biblical metaphor for describing Israel and the church is "the people of God." This hardly seems to be a metaphor in our context, but rather a statement describing a collection of individuals who belong to God. However, the true meaning of the word *people* in its original language and context is far more corporate; it is an ethnic or national reference. We might form a clearer picture if we translate it as "the nation of God." This clarifies the radical notion of this community being defined over and against earthly nations. "The people of God" refers to a contrast society set apart as a holy nation distinct from the political state of Israel (Deuteronomy 7:6-8). While this "people" is set apart from the world, it exists for the explicit purpose of blessing the world as a light to the nations.[5] This is not strictly a spiritual community, but one that acts in the world with a unique allegiance not to an earthly king but a heavenly one.

A sign, instrument, and foretaste of God's kingdom

More than anything else, Jesus proclaimed the presence of the kingdom of God, a kingdom marked by healing, reconciliation, justice, and peace. There is no indication that the church is the kingdom of God; they are distinct, yet intimately related. We discover implicitly and repeatedly in the Gospels that the church is a sign, instrument, and foretaste of the kingdom of God.[6]

As a sign, we point to something beyond ourselves. This means our proclamation and invitation always push beyond the physical walls of the church to announce reconciliation and redemption. In this way we are like the clouds before a storm, indicating something to come but also participating in the event itself. As an instrument we are like yeast in dough, active agents of God's kingdom. This means we participate in acts of healing, mercy, peace, and justice. As a foretaste we are like an appetizer before a feast. This means that in our worship and life we experience together brief glimpses of the abundant life in the Spirit.

The body of Christ

In 1 Corinthians 12:27, Paul tells us the church is the body of Christ. This metaphor calls the church to carry on the concrete, incarnational ministry of Jesus. Moreover, it is a call to community. The image of a physical body emphasizes that we are not simply a collection of individuals who share the same geography and believe the same things. This metaphor reminds us that the whole is greater than the sum of its parts. We are a corporate entity whose life and breath are derived from the dynamic interdependence of its people. The church is a living organism, not an institution of affiliated individuals.

Salt and light

In Matthew 5:13-14 Jesus tells us the church is the salt and light of the world. These metaphors remind us that the church doesn't have a mission—the church is a mission. Among other things, the images suggest the church represents a penetrating, contrasting way of living in the world—salt provides a penetrating taste, and light offers a contrast to darkness. These images stress the reality that the church is present in the world and at the same time quite different from it; we are strangers, but not strange. The unique contours of our community are what make us visible and penetrating. This uniqueness is derived as much from the way we interact with each other as from our personal piety. When our legitimate desire to be relevant and contextual leads to the wholesale adoption of our culture's methods, norms, and goals, we put our light under a bowl; we lose our saltiness.

The metaphors of salt and light are often seen as describing a call to personal witness—consider the words to "This Little Light of Mine." The words miss the corporate nature of the metaphor. These metaphors are directed at a community, not at individuals. When Jesus says, "You are the light of the world," it is a corporate image, not an individual one.

The original Greek text reveals this point better than English translations. When Jesus uses *you*, in "You are the light of the world," it is actually a plural form of the word, meaning "you all" or "you, yourselves" (or if you're from the South, "y'all"). The word *light* in the Greek is strikingly singular. Jesus uses a plural form of *you* but the singular form of *light*. He does not say, "You all are the *lights* of the world"; he says, "You all are the *light* of the world." We are not a thousand points of light; we are a corporate city on a hill.[7]

Thanks to the individualistic bias of the print age, we miss many of the biblical metaphors of the church because we assume these images are directed at individuals. This is especially true of Paul's epistles. But Paul was primarily concerned with forming communities; almost all of his letters are addressed to churches, not individuals. In fact, nearly everywhere in the Greek New Testament where Paul says "you," it is the plural "you all."

In 1 Corinthians 6:19-20 Paul writes, "Do you not know that your body is a temple of the Holy Spirit, who is in you, whom you have received from God? You are not your own; you were bought at a price. Therefore honor God with your body." For my entire Christian life I had understood this passage as a call to personal purity and individual morality. If I was ever tempted to drink or smoke growing up, I had these verses memorized as a cocked and ready defense. While I am grateful it warded off certain temptations, Paul is not talking about individual purity. He is talking about the church.

Every time Paul says "you" in this passage it is plural, yet every time he says "body" it is singular. He is speaking to a corporate group about their single body—*the church*. In this way, the church is the temple of the Holy Spirit, not me personally. Paul is emphasizing that the Spirit dwells in the corporate body as well as individual ones. While our individual purity matters, and I believe the Spirit dwells in us personally, this passage is actually concerned with the health of the community as a whole.

The true significance of this is understood well by a former seminary professor of mine. A Christian friend of his who was not a churchgoer approached him one day because this friend was struggling with a particular passage in one of Paul's epistles. This friend was intent on figuring out exactly what Paul was saying and what it meant for his life. After he laid out his dilemma, my professor responded by saying, "Don't worry about it." "What do you mean?" his friend replied. My professor explained, "You don't have to worry about it. It's not written to you; it was written for the church, and you're not part of a church, so you don't have to worry about it." His friend was a bit startled. My professor told me this man and his family joined a church soon after that conversation.

Whatever you think of my professor's tactics, the point he made is an important one. We need to read Scripture through a lens that is not just personal but also corporate. Instead of asking, "What does this passage mean to me?" we might ask, "What does this passage call our community to become?" When we begin to see the images in Scripture as corporate rather than individual, we can develop a more complete understanding of the true essence of the church and gain clarity on God's chosen medium.

DEVELOPING GUIDING METAPHORS FOR YOUR CHURCH

As we seek to recover our theology of the church, biblical metaphors are invaluable starting points, although not the final words. To understand the meaning of the church, we must be rooted in biblical meanings but continue to develop new metaphors that have relevance for our particular contexts. The true power of a metaphor is found in its ability to connect with culturally shared meanings. The image of a temple may not evoke shared meaning in a culture that has never seen one. And the metaphor of people doesn't even sound like a metaphor. So while it is important to understand the biblical images, we are invited to move beyond them to find images that will nurture shared meanings in our contexts.

This is already happening in many places. Following suit with the Graphic Revolution, emerging churches are increasingly employing metaphors to shape the identities of their local congregations. Refusing the standard naming conventions of a denominational designation (e.g., "First Baptist Church") or the generic community designation prefaced by a reference to nature (e.g., "Oakwood Community Church"), these emerging congregations are using metaphors to name their churches. Consider the names of just a few of these congregations: Journey, Garden, Tribe, Mosaic, New Ground, New Song, Solomon's Porch, Jacob's Well.

The metaphorical names evoke different ideas and images, some cryptic, others obvious. All are multilayered. Like biblical metaphors, some of these contemporary images seek to embody the mission and ethos of the congregations in single words. Yet because they are expressed as images rather than linguistic vision statements, they are open-ended enough to allow multiple levels of interpretation and multiple entry points for the congregants. The image of a garden may connote growth for some, beauty for others, or an organic structure for still others. All of these may be accurate, and yet none takes center stage. In this way new metaphors can help capture the dynamic and visionary nature of the body.

While there are great advantages to using metaphors, I am not suggesting churches throw out their existing names in favor of images. Nor do I claim that metaphors will solve all of our problems. But working with a collection of metaphors is a powerful way to develop shared meanings in a culture that uses concrete images to communicate.

When I started as a pastoral intern in my local congregation, we had just begun a long-range planning process. As a staff we were muddling through ideas about the best way to lead a diverse group of people toward a shared vision. We decided to experiment with images as a way to develop and describe our identity. As staff we explored biblical images of the church and then began working with a handful of these images as guiding metaphors for the congregation at large. These became the basis for a subsequent adult education and sermon series entitled "Images of the Church." This ensured that the congregation was part of the conversation, allowing people to feel they could fit in with the direction of the church. The flexible and dynamic nature of the metaphors provided multiple entry points for a diverse group of people.

This process helped us develop a shared language while allowing for some necessary diversity in meanings. Working with metaphors was not the ultimate solution to our problems; there were still plenty of difficulties in communicating and developing shared hopes and dreams. But it provided a useful rudder in an otherwise amorphous and unpredictable process.

THE CONSUMER-DRIVEN CHURCH: LOSING GOD'S MEDIUM

Exploring these metaphors and the nature of the church may feel unnecessary to some. It may feel like it's not all that complicated to be the church, to just live like Jesus. Yet understanding the church as the medium *and* the message is essential to maintaining our integrity as God's people, particularly as the church falls under the sway of our consumer culture.

At some point in the last half-century, advertisers stumbled upon the overwhelming power of images to manufacture needs and desires that don't naturally exist in humans. Over time this has helped create the juggernaut of consumer culture that penetrates nearly every aspect of our lives today. In the process, the church was blindsided as it was further stripped of its authority in society and became just another one of the many optional "lifestyle choices" available to consumers. Quite unexpectedly, the church was put in a position of having to compete for people's time, attention, and money. Those churches that resisted the shift by entrenching themselves in the past and attempting to reassert authority dwindled rapidly.

Other churches heeded consumer demands and sought to reinvent church. They realized they either had to compete in the consumer marketplace on the consumer's terms or face extinction. In the spirit of modernity, these churches reincarnated themselves as highly competent vendors of religious programs and services. Mirroring the techniques and structures of successful corporations, they employed sophisticated demographic and psychographic strategies for targeting consumers, implementing extensive marketing plans focused on meeting perceived needs of consumers sitting in the pews and at home. They developed extravagant weekend services designed to attract as many people as possible with the objective of maximizing individual transformation and deepening personal relationships with Jesus.

The results were stunning. Suburban consumers came in crowds, commuting great distances to attend these massive churches. Many of these churches are still thriving, and the echoes of triumph continue to resound throughout the evangelical world. As long as we live in a consumer society, these churches will continue to thrive. This mode of church has had a considerable impact on the lives of millions. Their leaders have a deep desire for people to know Christ and experience life transformations. Still, there has been little conversation about the ways in which the medium of the consumer-driven megachurch has shaped its message.

The medium of these churches is primarily a worship service designed to attract a crowd, respond to the overwhelming demands of a consumer society, and facilitate personal transformations. This way of doing church amplifies and reinforces the modern gospel that affirms individualism and the privatization of faith. Even though most of these churches put great emphasis on small groups—an effort to create intimate communities within the larger churches—the groups themselves tend to focus on personal faith and formation.

As a result, those who attend these churches gain a personal relationship with Jesus but are left with an impoverished theology of both community and the church. In this thoroughly modern, consumer-driven setting, church and community are valued, but only if they strengthen a Christian's personal relationship with Jesus. In this sense, community is little more than a tool. It is viewed simply as a tactical support mechanism for helping individuals better pursue their own private faiths.

This is in stark contrast to the biblical vision of the church in which individuals exist for the sake of the community and the community exists for God's mission in the world. God chose the *church*, not individual Christians, as the medium for mission. As we continue to face the issue of living the message (regardless of whether we understand it in a modern or postmodern context), our faithfulness to God's agenda demands we recover a theology of the church as a body sent as a foretaste of God's kingdom. In many ways this is at the heart of what is happening in the emerging church.

COMMUNITY IN ELECTRONIC CULTURE

CHAPTER SIX

At the time of my writing, two different phone companies launched a series of TV ads selling their mobile phone services. These ads illustrate an important truth about electronic culture. The first one, from AT&T, opens on a business traveler checking into a stark and lifeless motel room. He sits alone on the bed, appearing both dejected and lonely, wearing a somber look on his face. The ad then cuts to him sitting in an airport after his flight has been delayed. The music hobbles along to mirror the mood. A close-up of the man's face reveals an even more despairing look than he had in the motel room. But then something happens.

"THE IMMEDIATE PROSPECT FOR LITERATE, FRAGMENTED WESTERN MAN ENCOUNTERING THE ELECTRIC IMPLOSION… IS HIS…RAPID TRANSFORMATION INTO A COMPLEX… PERSON EMOTIONALLY AWARE OF HIS TOTAL INTERDEPENDENCE WITH THE REST OF HUMAN SOCIETY."[1]

"THE NEW ELECTRONIC INTERDEPENDENCE RE-CREATES THE WORLD IN THE IMAGE OF A GLOBAL VILLAGE."[2]

—MARSHALL MCLUHAN, 1964

Off-camera and out of nowhere we hear the sweet voice of a little girl saying, "Hi, Daddy." He turns to the seat next to him and his face immediately lights up. The scene cuts to a wide shot to reveal his five-year-old daughter now magically seated next to him. He is understandably thrilled, and they begin laughing and talking together. As they talk, the bustle of pedestrians obscures our view of the little girl and her dad. The moment the pedestrians pass, the scene has changed. The seat where his daughter was sitting is now empty, and he is once again alone. Only now he is talking on his cell phone, exuding the same elation as when his daughter was sitting next to him. The tag line says, "For the most important calls, reach out." The basic message is that AT&T's mobile phones can bridge great distances to bring you closer to the people you care about.

Nextel launched a different campaign. One of these ads opens on a wide shot of the altar at a wedding ceremony. We can see the bride, groom, and priest in position, but each is talking on a cell phone. A close-up reveals that the entire ritual is being mediated through cell phones even though the participants are standing inches from one another. The ceremony is performed with an efficiency that would make a NASCAR pit crew drool. The dialogue is expressed entirely through cell phones and goes like this:

> **Priest:** *[to groom]* "Do you?"
>
> **Groom:** "I do."
>
> **Priest:** *[to bride]* "Do you?"
>
> **Bride:** "I do."
>
> **Priest:** "Rings?"
>
> *[Bride and groom simultaneously flash rings affirmatively.]*
>
> **Priest:** "Kiss."
>
> *[Bride and groom make kissing sounds through their respective phones.]*
>
> **Priest:** "I pronounce you man and wife."
>
> *[Everyone cheers.]*

The ad ends with the tag line, "Nextel. Get it done." While the ad is touting the benefit of efficiency, every time I see this ad, I sit gazing at the TV with the curious head tilt of the RCA dog in front of the phonograph. This is because this ad, while attempting to highlight a benefit of cell phones, actually shows a hyperbole of a different truth. The truth is that while cell phones can bridge great distances and make us more efficient, they also have a tendency to isolate people even in close proximity.

Taken together, these ads reveal the paradoxical effect of mobile technology on our culture. It has a remarkable capacity to bring those far away much closer (AT&T) while at the same time making those near us much farther away (Nextel). Since I've had e-mail, I have far more contact with friends thousands of miles away—I would say we are closer because of it. At the same time, I have a friend who lives two doors down from us, and I am more inclined to e-mail him than I am to walk next door and talk with him face to face. This paradox is at the heart of the challenges we face in forming community in an electronic age.

A TRIBE OF INDIVIDUALS

As we've seen, electronic culture isn't exactly new. Much of it borrows from both the oral and print eras. In fact, electronic media creates a paradoxical hybrid of the two previous communication cultures.[3] If the oral world was primarily tribal or communal in nature, and the print age was individualistic, then electronic culture has turned us into a tribe of individuals. This paradox, among others, limits and expands the way we form community in an electronic age. It is a phenomenon breeding new tensions and traumas in our world where people are pulled in two directions at the same time.

As discussed in Chapter Four, certain media in the electronic age, such as radio and TV, have a retribalizing power in that they have a tendency to return us to certain aspects of oral culture. Most powerfully, they retrieve a group experience and reverse the private individualism of the print age. An individual is defined in part by a set of experiences unique to that person. Radio and TV profoundly minimize these unique experiences. People do not have a unique point of view when they experience an event via television. Instead, viewers experience an event through the same set of camera angles at the same moment as millions of other viewers. In this way, TV causes individual experience to give way to group experience.

Consider the tragedy of September 11, 2001. The millions of us who watched the catastrophic events on TV witnessed the same event at the same moment from exactly the same camera angles—this was a group experience, not one experienced from a unique point of view. In fact, it was such a uniform mass experience that there was no need to recount what I saw to a friend across the country—he saw the same event from exactly the same perspective. I was far more interested to hear the stories of three of my friends who were near Ground Zero and witnessed these events directly and uniquely.

Our culture has been participating in these mass tribal experiences for over a century. One result of these group experiences is a greater awareness of our total interdependence on the rest of humanity. This global tribe is also breeding a cultural fascination with more communal ways of living. The fragmentary individualism of the print age has slowly dissolved under the unifying and retribalizing power of TV.

REALITY TV AND THE NEW "TRIBALISM"

This existential shift toward community was first discernible in the late 1960s with a burgeoning number of experiments in which people created intentional communities or communes where they sought to share common possessions and living space. Not coincidentally, these experiments began shortly after television had become a near-universal household appliance in the late 1950s.[4]

When these intentional community experiments started, they occurred mostly among marginal groups in society, not in the mainstream. However, the fascination with community continued and now exists in the broader population. This longing can be seen in the popularity of so-called "reality TV." It is often observed that this genre plays upon and reveals the voyeuristic appetites of our culture. But this is not voyeurism. Voyeurism occurs when we gain enjoyment from watching people who don't know they are being watched. With reality TV, nothing could be further from the truth; the players are not only aware that they are being watched, but they are also counting on it. These shows actually reveal a different cultural appetite, one which is rarely talked about. They demonstrate an intense curiosity with community and tribal living.

The most successful reality TV shows in the last decade have shared a common element. It began with MTV's *The Real World* in the early 1990s and has been used more recently by shows like *Survivor*, *Big Brother*, and even *The Apprentice*. The common ingredient? Forced cohabitation.

These shows place people in situations where they are forced to live as a tribe. In a culture that remains highly individualistic yet is constantly participating in the group experience of electronic culture, we've become fascinated by how people actually live together in such close proximity. Very few of us are aware that this is what we tune in for, but the creators know this better than anyone.

An estimated 40 million people tune in every week to watch these unscripted dramas. The show *Survivor* marooned contestants on a remote island, thereby depriving them of personal luxuries and modern amenities and forcing a return to tribal living. The drama of the show emerged out of the clash of individualized people forced to live amidst the intensely invasive social relations of a literal tribe.

In the show *The Apprentice,* contestants compete to become the next CEO for one of Donald Trump's many companies. While this takes place in the heart of Manhattan, it might surprise some to learn that its creator intentionally engineered a remarkably similar kind of tribal living as seen on *Survivor*. Contestants are forced to live together, prohibited from watching TV, listening to music, reading newspapers, or getting on the Internet (unless it is for business purposes), and limited in their phone privileges.[5] In other words, not only do they live together, but they are also stranded on a first-world urban island with restricted access to typical technological distractions. This means they are forced to interact with one another, ensuring conflict.

What is most telling about our culture is that the popularity of these shows is achieved without well-written scripts, violence, or even secret twists. Our electronic culture has a keen interest in the drama that ensues from community living.

THE THEOLOGY OF COMMUNITY

This cultural shift toward community can also be seen in the evangelical theology of the last few decades. Evangelical theologians are going back to Scripture and mining it for a more communal approach to the life of faith. In the introduction to *Theology for the Community of God* (a systematic theology textbook), Stanley J. Grenz writes that his goal is "to consider our faith within the context of God's central program for creation, namely, the establishment of community."[6] Miroslav Volf, in his book *After Our Likeness: The Church as the Image of the Trinity*, describes a theology of the church that is reflective of and rooted deeply in the communitarian fellowship of the Trinity.[7]

The list of books reviving a theology of community goes on; clearly, evangelical theology is awakening from the age of the private individual into a new preference for community. This marks a shift away from small group ministries as little more than tools designed to aid and support our private faith. Instead, as we shall see, some churches are developing a more radical theology of community in which we exist for the community and the life of faith cannot be known apart from the gathered people of God. Community comes from deliberately choosing to live near one another rather than developing from a structured meeting with a set curriculum. Faith is still personal, but no longer private.

Once again, this shift can be connected to the move from our modern worldview to the postmodern worldview ushered in during the electronic age. If the modern era of print caused an explosion that fragmented the Western world into a collection of private individuals, the electronic era has done the opposite. It has caused an implosion, throwing individuals together with a force never seen before. While some have responded to this implosion with a heightened desire for privacy (as evidenced by the growth in gated communities and houses on enormous lots meant to give a sense of separation from neighbors), others have moved in the opposite direction, intentionally giving up private space in order to gain a sense of intimate community with others.

However, while the efforts at building intentional community have continued from the 1960s until today, experts estimate that nearly 90 percent of these intentional communities in North America fail.[8] I have personally known half a dozen people who enthusiastically entered into intentional communities and left shortly after to recover from what they described as emotionally invasive experiences. This isn't to say healthy community is impossible; I also know many people for whom community living is preferred. My wife and I have lived intentionally with others and had positive experiences. But clearly something isn't working right if the failure rate is so high.

My belief is that despite the retribalizing force of electronic media, our culture remains intensely individualistic. Electronic media have not done away with the individualizing forces of literacy and printing entirely. Literacy rates remain very high in the West. We are still readers; consider the *Left Behind* series, which has sold an estimated 62 million copies,[9] or the *Harry Potter* books, which have sold upwards of 45 million. Even a nonfiction book like Rick Warren's *The Purpose-Driven Life* has sold over 20 million copies.

The age of print no longer reigns supreme, but we cannot chisel an epitaph on its tombstone just yet. Its legacy is deeply embedded in our cultural history and not likely to die anytime soon. America is the only country in history to be argued into existence via the printed word. Thus from its earliest inception, much of our cultural ideology was shaped by the power of printing. The First Amendment to the United States Constitution claims an inherent right to intellectual freedom, private judgment, and individuality. These notions are derived directly from the ideological biases of the printed word.[10] Moreover, our entire educational system is predicated on the mastery of reading and writing. As long as this educational emphasis remains, our culture will continue to have modern individualism woven into the very fiber of our identities. We are formed as private individuals in this culture from very early on.

ELECTRONIC NOMADS: FROM INDIVIDUALISM TO ISOLATION

Not only are we constituted as individuals by literacy and our country's history, but our individualism is also reinforced by certain aspects of electronic media. While some electronic media inspire a tribal impulse, others are separating us from the tribe—this is the paradox noted earlier. In addition to their tendency both to bring people together and pull us apart, cell phones, e-mail, PDAs, and other mobile devices have another push/pull effect. While they connect us to more people, more often, from greater distances than ever before—meaning we no longer need to share geography with others to have community—they have caused us to lose our sense of place.[11]

Increasingly, we have become electronic nomads—people whose electronic locations are in constant flux. When I talk on the phone with someone in Europe, my voice is disembodied, and electronically I am in Europe. I am no longer fully present in my physical location. While it may seem insignificant, this lack of presence is important. Consider the phenomenon that it is more dangerous to drive a car while talking on a hands-free cell phone than to drive while talking with a friend sitting next to you. When talking on a cell phone, a person is simply not fully present in the car. Cell phones and the like reduce us to partly disembodied souls electronically residing in other locations. In this sense, electronic technology can have an isolating, fragmenting effect.

As electronic nomads, we experience other strange paradoxes and hybrids of previous eras. If tribal culture is intensely connected or empathic and print culture is more distant, then our electronic experience creates *empathy at a distance*.[12] When famines, wars, and natural disasters halfway around the world flicker through the TV in my living room, they evoke an empathic response; my heart goes out to those suffering. In this sense, TV extends my emotions. It connects me to human suffering on a global scale and also makes me keenly aware of my relative peace, prosperity, and provision.

One positive effect of TV's capacity to extend our emotional experiences became clear in the 1960s when the civil rights movement gained popular support in the North, primarily because TV exposed the horror and injustice of white police officers bruising the bodies of defenseless black citizens with fire hoses. The public outrage over this situation provided President Kennedy with a necessary mandate from the masses to take initiative to end segregation.

This is the positive power of electronic media. However, like all media, when pushed to an extreme, electronic media can reverse into an opposite effect. The experience of empathy at a distance doesn't always motivate us to act. In fact, when we are exposed to too many traumatic experiences all at once, it actually has a numbing effect on the psyche. This numbness is the mind's way of keeping legitimate feelings of helplessness and hopelessness at bay. We then become far less likely to engage in God's mission to bring reconciliation and healing to the world.

COTTON CANDY COMMUNITY: SPOILING OUR APPETITE

As electronic nomads, we do not sojourn as a group—we drift and journey on our own. However, we are hardly aware of this aloneness because we are constantly participating in a network of other disembodied acquaintances and loved ones. This is one reason the AT&T father-daughter commercial is so seductive. The ad suggests that a cell phone can make up for a lack of face-to-face interactions. Most of us know this is not true, but the ad seeks to dull our awareness by making us believe buying a cell phone is the appropriate and efficient response to our culture's overwhelming mobility, fragmentation, and isolation. An alternative response would be to get a different job that pays less and keeps Dad closer to home. However, our culture does not reward those who rein in the concentric circles of their lives; such an option is seen as both naive and unrealistic. Yet this may be the very response the gospel calls us to consider.

Our virtual relationships have a strange effect. They provide just enough of a connection to paralyze our best efforts at unmediated community. In virtual community, our contacts involve very little real risk and demand even less of us personally. In this sense, we experience the paradox of *intimate anonymity*. We have the illusion of being intimate with people while remaining totally anonymous if we desire—this is the draw and danger of Internet chat rooms. There is no need to offer real vulnerability. Community that promises freedom from rejection and makes authentic emotional investment optional can be extremely appealing, remarkably efficient, and a lot more convenient.

In this way, a virtual or electronic community functions a bit like cotton candy: it goes down easy and satiates our immediate hunger, but it doesn't provide much in the way of sustainable nutrition. It spoils our appetite for the kind of authentic community to which Scripture calls us.

"Authentic community" is an elusive and slippery term. Borrowing from sociologists and theologians, I share the assumption that authentic community involves high degrees of intimacy, permanence, and proximity. These practices foster shared memories as well as a shared imagination of the future, elements crucial to becoming the people of God.[13] While relative intimacy can be gained in virtual settings, the experiences of permanence and proximity have all but vanished. Without these, we lose our shared memories and imagination for where we are going, elements central to our identity as God's people.

If virtual community functions like cotton candy, then authentic community is more like broccoli. It may not always taste good but it provides crucial nourishment for the formation of our identity. Authentic community will undoubtedly be marked by conflict, risk, and rejection. At the same time it offers the deepest levels of acceptance, intimacy, and support.

I'm not morally opposed to cotton candy. It serves a legitimate, albeit limited, function in one's diet. In the same way, I am not morally opposed to virtual community; it also serves an important and limited function in our electronic culture. The problem is that virtual community is slowly becoming the preferred means of relating, even in the church. I have known many people with subtle addictions to virtual community such as chat rooms or weblogs ("blogs"). I have two friends in particular who live no more than two miles apart. They connect several times a day via cell phone but rarely meet face to face. They consider themselves the closest of friends, but both have lamented to me on separate occasions that they know very little of each other's deepest struggles and desires; it remains a somewhat superficial relationship. They are quite unaware of the cell phone's power to inoculate our need to connect in person, which is where true intimacy and depth are born.

Blogs, when taken to an extreme, present a related problem. They allow us to participate in organic dialogue. However, they also have a remarkably addictive tendency to tickle our intellects, seducing us into a Pandora's box of perpetual links, people, and ideas. The result is that we are drawn wider but rarely deeper. This is true both in terms of the ideas we explore and the relationships we build. The great wonder of blogging is found in its dynamic speed. We are exposed to many more ideas than previously possible, and we are given a chance to dialogue about them in near real-time settings. However, the medium of blogging, regardless of content, has a natural bias toward confusion rather than clarity. It prefers careless language patterns, slack logic, and superficial relationships. This is at the expense of intellectual precision, thoughtful language, and meaningful connection with those in close proximity.

Churches have begun to use blogs, chat areas, and electronic bulletin boards in their efforts to build community. Yet there remains the danger of people finding connection through these electronic forms and believing they have found genuine intimacy. This can cause them to miss out on authentic community with the people they worship with each week.

We must develop an awareness of our unconscious tendency to be seduced by our virtual communities so we can use them more intentionally rather than be used by them. Our subtle addiction to electronic community is not like an addiction to drugs where the only solution is to stop using entirely. It is more like an addiction to food or money, where we must learn to regain power over something we cannot do without. We need to develop healthy relationships with our technologies. This means nurturing a conscious awareness of their power, our longings, and the way both of these shape us. On occasion we may consider fasting from certain media as a spiritual discipline. This can be a very effective way to help us perceive media's power and recalibrate our psyches.

THE DIFFERENCE BETWEEN BEING "IN TOUCH" AND IN COMMUNITY

This addiction to virtual community is quite understandable. It is just too convenient not to participate. We love the efficiency of our interactions; they allow us to be in touch more often. However, there is a big difference between being "in touch" and truly connecting with others. I discovered this, strangely enough, during my time in the business world.

I had a particular role that depended heavily upon people in several other departments. Most of the people I worked with were scattered throughout the building. Early in my career I learned people in my role did their jobs primarily by shooting off e-mails to the relevant parties in other departments detailing their requests and noting deadlines. E-mail, they said, was a lifesaver; it was so much more efficient, and it was always better to have your requests in writing so you wouldn't later get blamed for unclear communication.

I mirrored this method but found the responses to my requests to be slow in coming. More often than not I would physically have to track down the people and negotiate a solution to the problem at hand. When I did, they would dig their heels in and exude dispositions of being profoundly inconvenienced at my need for them to do their jobs. I also discovered my own departmental colleagues spending their lunch hours commiserating about the total lack of helpfulness in other departments. Apparently, this was an issue for everyone. The other departments just weren't team players.

This was all happening at about the time I was learning how media and technology shape us. In the midst of my learning I decided to try an experiment. For two weeks I decided only to make my project requests in person. I would sit down in other people's offices; inevitably, we would carry on inefficient conversations about non-work-related matters and eventually discuss my project needs. It was often difficult to find people, and I spent a lot of time walking around the building, looking for my colleagues. It felt like a lot more work to do it this way, and initially, it took longer—but I found there to be a number of benefits.

As deadlines approached, people from other departments actually came to find me to deliver my requests in person, and I encountered none of the typical resistance. I also discovered they worked on my projects before they worked on my colleagues' e-mail requests, even those requests with tighter deadlines. Our face-to-face meetings built a relationship in a way e-mail could not. These relationships made all the difference in making both of our jobs more enjoyable. It was somewhat inefficient at first, and I was in contact with them less frequently, but our face-to-face connections were more meaningful and effective in the long run.

A few years later I learned my personal experiment had been done on a larger scale by professors at Stanford Business School. They focused on business negotiations made face to face, over the telephone, and via e-mail. Not surprisingly, they found that negotiations performed exclusively over e-mail broke down far more often than face-to-face or even telephone negotiations.[14]

It sounds almost too obvious to say, but personal connections have an immeasurable impact on how we establish, build, and maintain relationships. While most of us know this already, it's amazing how few of us practice it. The experience of virtual community can feel just as real as physical community, but the social, spiritual, and emotional realities do not provide the same kind of connections. This means we must be discerning about the way we use information technologies to make decisions or build and maintain relationships in the church. We must ask how our media change personal interactions. We need to consider the message conveyed when we choose e-mail contact over a personal visit, a phone call, or a handwritten note. These may seem like mundane questions, but they help generate an awareness of the forces that inhibit and build community.

MOVING BEYOND INDIVIDUALISM

The challenge of forming and staying in community in electronic culture goes beyond issues of increased mobility afforded by the newest technologies. It has a great deal to do with how our identity is formed at an early age. In a purely tribal culture, identity is derived almost entirely from the complex interplay of relationships that comprise the tribe. The question of "Who am I apart from the community?" is almost never considered. In an individualistic culture, identity is determined in part by discovering the ways we are unique. We learn very early on to develop boundaries to mark the place where others end and we begin. We demand our privacy (which, thanks to printing, is our birthright in America) and seek to protect our personal spaces. This is a unique part of our cultural gifting as well as our sickness. Our staunch individualism is so central to our identities that we find it difficult to live in the kind of community to which Scripture calls us. However, we should not consider our failure at or lack of desire for community living simply as sin or selfishness to be overcome.

The fact that most intentional communities fail reveals the profound difficulty experienced by highly individualized people attempting to live life as a tribe. A culture conditioned by individualism is not formed in such a way to withstand the intensely invasive social relations of tribal living. Developing boundaries and having privacy aren't just something we prefer in this culture: they are integral to our emotional and psychological health. Our goal as Christian communities should not be to undo this, but to work within our limitations and gifts as they are.

The starting point for doing so begins, paradoxically, by respecting the reality of our need for privacy and the boundaries that comprise our identity. Only after we respect these realities can we be invited to relinquish *voluntarily* certain privacy rights to those we trust. Only then can we be invited to renegotiate some of our more rigid boundaries and open ourselves to the risk of life together.

A variety of structures can be used to facilitate greater communal faith in our context. No single model is going to be right for every person's unique emotional and spiritual identity blend. However, there is at least one practical example that seeks to balance a respect for individualism with a desire to move into deeper life with others. It's called cohousing (learn more at www.cohousing.org).

THE COHOUSING COMMUNITY

This community-building movement is burgeoning on the fringes of our culture and is often more sustainable and stable than previous attempts at intentional community. Cohousing is a type of collaborative living that migrated from Denmark in the late 1980s.

It is characterized by a group of smaller, self-sufficient private residences organized around extensive common facilities—typically a large dining room, kitchen, recreational room, etc. The architecture is intentionally designed to encourage more frequent social contact but still respect privacy needs. This type of housing is developed and managed by residents who share a conscious commitment to community living. While the practices of the communities vary widely, these communities typically share at least one meal a week in their common space as well as contribute to maintaining the property.

This is a powerful way to learn what it means to live together and still keep one's own space. My friends who live in settings like this have overcome much of the isolation in our culture and have developed deep wells of hospitality. They are not afraid to heed our gospel call to welcome the stranger and outsider. This is in part because they know what it means to be welcomed and have a web of friendships in close proximity who share the risks and burdens of living in intimate community.

Naturally, cohousing represents a more radical approach to developing community than most of us would be willing to consider. I do not share it as a model for everyone, but the model becomes an important object lesson. Whatever structures or forms we choose, they must work toward developing healthy communities that acknowledge our individualism and still invite us to live beyond ourselves.

Smaller steps can also be taken to help develop the kind of interdependent community we are called to. Some of my most challenging and profound encounters in community have come as a result of experimenting with new ways of building relationships. For example, my wife and I have intentionally built relationships with people in our church. We have invited these people to be involved in major decisions in our life, whether job transitions, where we live, or even financial issues. These people are not simply sounding boards who have marginal places in our decisions. They have special permission to speak into our lives, ask hard questions, and challenge our thinking. We consider their feedback to be more than just other opinions. Theirs are the most important opinions. We have an informal covenant in which they agree to be mindful of their own agendas and open to the Spirit's prompting. For our part, we agree to take their input solemnly and listen carefully for the Spirit in their reflections, questions, and challenges.

In many ways such a covenant stands in direct contradiction to the American model of autonomous individualism. On those occasions when we have wanted to go in one direction and they invited us in another, we have felt that tension deeply. Yet in every case, we have developed deeper intimacy, connection, and honesty because of this covenant. More than once I was confronted by my own selfishness, lack of faith, and underlying fears. Remarkably, the interactions with this community were the catalysts that freed me from these things and birthed new hope and trust. This would not have occurred without deliberately nurturing these relationships.

Relationships like these require both sacrifice and submission in which we voluntarily give the community authority to help shape the way we live. Doing so has allowed these friendships to take on a missional quality, as our interactions serve as signposts to others that mark the upside-down ways of God's kingdom.

STORYTELLING AS A CATALYST FOR COMMUNITY

As you might imagine, such trusted and intimate relationships take time, commitment, and proximity to develop. Fortunately, the church is uniquely suited to helping us develop such relationships. One of the most powerful ways to deepen our connections is the practice of storytelling as a corporate spiritual discipline.

This can be done in a variety of ways. One congregation I know began encouraging the process in their small groups. Each week, two members of the small group were asked to prepare a written autobiography to share with the group. The focus of their stories was narrowed to a specific subject like a spiritual autobiography, a family autobiography, or a vocational autobiography in which they would share their histories on these specific subjects.

Perhaps the most potent subject for these communities was something they called the "money autobiography." For this assignment, presenters were asked to write about their best and worst memories related to money. They were asked to reflect on their hopes, fears, and sadnesses related to finances. They were to recount the teachings they received concerning money from their families, their culture, or their friends. They were asked to make connections with Scripture when possible.

In one of the groups at least one presenter would show up each week with credit cards in hand and say, "Please hold these for me.

I'm in too much debt; I need help." The effect on the group was profound, as it caused them to reconsider the role money played in their discipleship to Christ. They learned about the ways our culture of wealth breeds secrecy and privacy around issues of money. They became aware of the erosive power this kind of secrecy had on their relationships with one another.

These people were never asked to tithe more, reveal their net worth, or hand over their credit cards. And yet the process nurtured a more generous community. The changes in their lives took place when they were given space to tell and hear each other's stories. It developed new openness, trust, and intimacy.

LEARNING TO LIVE WITH CONFLICT

The immediate challenge for those of us living in electronic culture is the force by which electronic media has thrown us together and torn us apart. In this sense, the global implosion presents us with opportunities for interpersonal conflict unlike anything we are accustomed to. As we experiment with more authentic forms of community, we will experience levels of conflict we are simply not used to. As a result, we need to find resources to help us navigate the reality of increasing conflict when attempting to live life together.

Scripture provides us with just such a resource. Of the many commands Jesus gave, two are of particular importance here: one is the call to love our neighbors as ourselves, and the other is the call to love our enemies. Perhaps the most powerful truth behind the two commands is that these two people groups (neighbors and enemies) are not all that different. Our neighbors, those closest to us, have great potential to become our enemies. Andy Crouch puts it best when he writes, "No one gets out of any serious experiment in human community—church, marriage, family, or otherwise—without discovering, and becoming, an enemy."[15] This is an inevitable and uncomfortable consequence of living in such close proximity with our boundaries repeatedly pressed and challenged. Yet we are called to it.

Tribal cultures are quite accustomed to this style of relating. For an individualistic culture, however, conflict is typically viewed as a bad thing, something to be minimized and avoided if possible. Unfortunately, conflict doesn't go away simply because it is unwelcome or feared. Rather it finds other, more insidious ways to disrupt communities. It quickly finds a home in the shadowy back alleys of relationships. Without a climate of open conflict, diagnosing problems in the community, let alone dealing with them, becomes nearly impossible. When we learn to welcome conflict as a natural and healthy part of human community, we can dispel some of its power to be destructive. In fact, under the right circumstances, conflict can be a powerful means of growth and intimacy.

As we learn to weave our lives together as a community, it is imperative that we accept conflict as a given and welcome it as an integral part of our corporate health. One way to learn how to do this constructively is by developing an explicit theology of conflict for our communities.

A helpful resource for this task can be found in the Anabaptist stream of faith. The Anabaptists have a robust theology of conflict. It is accepted as a given and forms an important foundation of their communal life. This is true for two reasons. First, they have a long tradition of concretely living out their faith in tightly bound intentional communities. Second, they practice nonviolence and have long struggled with what it means to deal with conflict peaceably. As a consequence, they know better than most of us what it means to accept our enemies as our neighbors and still live peaceably.

As we begin to experiment and practice a more communal approach to faith, it is helpful to listen to the wisdom of these kinds of communities. To help us do so, I have included an excerpt from a document used as a pledge or covenant for Mennonite churches.

AGREEING AND DISAGREEING IN LOVE

COMMITMENTS FOR MENNONITES IN TIMES OF DISAGREEMENT

"Making every effort to maintain the unity of the Spirit in the bond of peace," (Ephesians 4:3) as *both individual members and the body of Christ, we pledge that we shall:*

In Thought

1. *Accept conflict*—acknowledge together that conflict is a normal part of our life in the church (Romans 14:1-8, 10-12, 17-19; 15:1-7).

2. *Affirm hope*—affirm that as God walks with us in conflict, we can work through to growth (Ephesians 4:15-16).

3. *Commit to prayer*—admit our needs and commit ourselves to pray for a mutually satisfactory solution (no prayers for my success or for the other to change but to find a joint way) (James 5:16).

In Action

4. *Go to the other…*—go directly to those with whom we disagree; avoid behind-the-back criticism (Matthew 5:23-24; 18:15-20).

5. *…in the spirit of humility*—go in gentleness, patience, and humility. Place the problem between us at neither doorstep and own our part in the conflict instead of pointing out others' (Galatians 6:1-5).

6. *Be quick to listen*—listen carefully, summarize, and check out what is heard before responding. Seek as much to understand as to be understood (James 1:19; Proverbs 18:13).

7. *Be slow to judge*—suspend judgments, avoid labeling, end name calling, discard threats, and act in a nondefensive, nonreactive way (Romans 2:1-4; Galatians 5:22-26).

8. *Be willing to negotiate*—work through the disagreements constructively, celebrate small agreements along the way, cooperate with the emerging agreement (Acts 15; Philippians 2:1-11).

In Life

9. *Be steadfast in love*—be firm in our commitment to seek a mutual solution; be stubborn in holding to our common foundation in Christ; be steadfast in love (Colossians 3:12-15).

10. *Be open to mediation*—be open to accept skilled help. If we cannot reach agreement among ourselves, we will use those with gifts and training in mediation in the larger church (Philippians 4:1-3).

11. *Trust the community*—we trust the community, and if we cannot reach agreement or experience reconciliation, we will turn the decision over to others in the congregation or from the broader church (Acts 15).

12. *Be the body of Christ*—believe in and rely on the solidarity of the body of Christ and its commitment to peace and justice, rather than resort to the courts of law (1 Corinthians 6:1-6)

Perhaps the most groundbreaking aspect of this Mennonite document is the first point: "Accept conflict." With this simple statement they turn a potentially destructive force at work in the body of Christ into a powerfully constructive one. As Mennonite theologian John Howard Yoder puts it, "To be human is to be in conflict, to offend and to be offended. To be human in light of the gospel is to face conflict in redemptive dialogue."[16]

Very little of this approach to conflict resolution is groundbreaking. In fact, all of the ideas are as old as Scripture. While this document is a helpful resource, this is not the only way to deal with conflict. This represents an excellent model for a particular community and approach to faith. For other contexts conflict resolution might look quite different. The point I want to stress is not the specifics, but the notion that the health of our communities can be aided by incorporating an open, robust, and practical theology of conflict.

GO THEREFORE AND MAKE...COMMUNITY?

It is strange that we spend so much time and energy on the issue of creating community. After all, Jesus tells us to make disciples, not communities. Jesus came proclaiming eternal life and the kingdom of God, not community. And yet community is an implicit assumption throughout the Bible. Community is the soil out of which the flower of discipleship grows. A corporate understanding of the gospel was simply assumed until the individualism of the print age stripped the gospel of its corporate and communal meanings.

Our call to community is not simply a call to find support groups to help with daily living or aid our personal faith journeys. Although this is a legitimate and important by-product of community, the call to community isn't just for the benefit of the individual. We exist for the community, and the community exists for God and God's purposes. God has chosen to use a corporate witness to embody and announce the kingdom on earth.

As a tribe of individuals pulled in two directions, we may find living this out to be quite difficult. Our electronic media has rekindled our interest in community and made us aware of our total interdependence on one another even as it has increased our mobility, isolation, and individualism. In our quest for meaningful connections we encounter convenient decoys—the always-appealing cotton candy communities of the virtual world.

Scripture calls us to something more. It invites us to move beyond our mobility, computer screens, and cell phones to participate in authentic community marked by proximity and permanence, shared memories, and corporate dreams for the future. This is not a call to renounce our individualism, nor is it a rejection of technology; we are simply not capable of doing either in this culture. Instead, we begin with a healthy respect for our individualism accompanied by gentle invitations to move beyond it. We learn to understand the power of our technologies to shape us, thereby regaining power over them.

Entering into authentic community means more conflict where we meet our neighbors as our enemies. It also leads to a deepening of personal support while at the same time strengthening our corporate mission to be a penetrating contrast society of salt and light. Finally, it means becoming the people of God and the body of Christ.

LEADERSHIP IN ELECTRONIC CULTURE

CHAPTER SEVEN

It was my junior year in college, and I had technically been elected as the president of the Christian fraternity on campus. I use the word *technically* because, in all fairness, I ran for this office unopposed. Nonetheless, my peers granted me the role of leading the fraternity and overseeing the other four elected officers. In an effort to prepare for my new role I sought the counsel of two former presidents of the fraternity who were still around. I wanted to know how they went about leading a team of their peers.

"CHRISTIANITY—IN A CENTRALIZED, ADMINISTRATIVE, BUREAUCRATIC FORM—IS CERTAINLY IRRELEVANT."[1]

"WE MUST GET RID OF THE HIERARCHY [IN THE CHURCH] IF WE WANT PARTICIPATION. BUT WE DON'T HAVE TO WISH FOR IT. IT'S HAPPENING."[2]

—MARSHALL MCLUHAN, 1970

One of them shared the following: "As president I never really liked the image of me being 'above' the other officers. I didn't consider myself as the head of the totem pole. I preferred the idea that we were all equal members of a team." He went on to describe a collaborative and participatory style of leadership in which he renounced much of his positional authority in the interest of empowering the other team members. He didn't create a vision and communicate it; instead he allowed a vision to emerge from the team. I left that meeting grateful for his input, but frankly I wasn't impressed. It struck me as a rather bland and impotent leadership style. *Maybe he was just too afraid to assert himself,* I thought.

The other former president gave me a different perspective. He had a strong sense of vision and imagined himself as a trailblazer who led with all the authority the position granted him. His job was to be the creator, keeper, and dispenser of the vision. He was clearly in charge of the other officers and felt responsible for their performance. As president he was a one-man show. He would take counsel from his officers, but it was clear the decisions were his to make. At the end of this meeting I felt inspired. His style seemed stronger, more forward-looking, and impressive. I decided to imitate that style as best I could. As I got into the position, I found that some of this came naturally to me, while at other times it felt forced and a bit self-inflating. Nonetheless, I was the president and I assumed this was how strong leaders acted.

When it comes to leadership in the church, both of these styles are well represented. I do not believe either style should be universally applied in every situation. Rather, each is appropriate for different contexts and occasions. That said, I think I was wrong in my original assessments. I initially thought the more collaborative style was weak and driven more by fear than by a sense of fairness. Today I believe such a style requires a leader with considerable strength, self-knowledge, and self-confidence. Moreover, I have also come to believe the centralized command and control style of leadership should not be our default setting. This style of leadership is increasingly outmoded and has a tendency to be dangerous for the health of both pastors and congregations in a postmodern context.

THE CHANGING IMAGES OF LEADERSHIP IN THE EMERGING CHURCH

Many leaders in the emerging church find institutional and centralized hierarchies to be irrelevant and even dangerous. They argue that such structures have too much power for their own good and are simply not mobile enough to respond to perpetual changes in culture. The metaphors for this kind of church leadership often include images like the CEO or the resident expert. These images tend to separate and elevate the pastor as distinct from the people of God. Authority and control then become more top-down and static with little internal accountability—much as in the business world.

Emerging churches have taken a steamroller to hierarchies in favor of more collaborative and participatory models of leadership. In these settings, the pastor becomes one among equals; Spencer Burke uses the metaphor of pastors as "fellow travelers" rather than "tour guides."[3] It is a team-based approach to leadership comprised of people who partner with one another on equal footing. Such leaders may not have all the answers or all the power. Instead, they are integrated into the life and community of the congregation.

The descriptions above give us a window into the changing nature of leadership in the emerging church. However, behind these shifting attitudes are changes in the way our culture feels about authority. It is crucial that we understand these shifts to make sense of new leadership structures in the church today. As I have already argued, postmodern attitudes in general are brought about in part by our electronic media, regardless of content. These new media forms shape the way we think and interact with the world. Our shifting attitudes toward authority are no exception; they are partly the result of our electronic media. Again, electronic media are not the *only* causes of cultural changes—they are just the most often overlooked.

Our changing attitudes about leadership have a great deal to do with our feelings and beliefs about authority. It has long been observed that youth in the 1960s—the boomer generation—began to have a suspicious attitude toward authority. Distrust for institutions and government became the norm. Such suspicion has only intensified in the emerging generation and is directly related to our media habits.

There is a simple explanation for this: Authority is often derived from information control. In other words, as access to information increases, centralized authority decreases. Whenever people have exclusive access to information, they are granted a certain degree of authority, which is why doctors, lawyers, and mechanics receive such deference and why IT employees in corporate America often have more authority than CEOs. However, changes in communication technologies often serve to erode the barriers to information, making it more accessible and, in the process, changing power dynamics.[4] The same thing is happening in the church. As theological information is now more accessible than ever (i.e., online Bible commentaries, theologian blogs, etc.), the Protestant church hierarchy is collapsing.

THE CENTRALIZATION OF THE CHURCH

The church has a long history of hierarchical leadership structures, but it wasn't always that way. The early church was much more egalitarian. The reason for this change has everything to do with media. In a purely oral culture, everyone has the same information. Since there is no place to store information outside the mind, these cultures spend time telling and retelling stories as the chief means of retaining them. In this situation, power is dispersed throughout the tribe, because everyone shares the same basic information. Although the early church did have some manuscripts in circulation, they had not developed a sacred view of these texts—in theory, they were available to anyone. So the early church functioned in ways similar to an oral culture; information and thus authority tended to be shared.

However, once the New Testament writings were officially compiled by A.D. 367 and deemed sacred, an elite scribal or priestly class discovered they had tremendous authority, because they had exclusive access to a limited number of manuscripts containing sacred information. They alone possessed the skills for decoding these texts. Here we see the catalyst that allowed the institutional medieval Catholic Church to place power and authority in the hands of priests and popes.

The Shift in Authority

This centralized, hierarchical authority emerged gradually after the compilation of the New Testament and continued until the Protestant Reformation in the 1500s, when the printing press introduced cracks in the information dam between the priestly class and the public. In the 1500s information began slowly seeping through these cracks in the wall. Latin, Greek, and Hebrew manuscripts were finally translated into the vernacular languages of the European people (i.e., French, Spanish, English, and German), giving the public direct access to these sacred texts in an infinitely repeatable form. Now people had access to God's Word in their own languages.

It was only a matter of time until people developed the levels of literacy necessary to access the sacred information on their own.

Authority was no longer derived exclusively from control of information. Instead it diffused to those who had knowledge of the Bible, a capacity for rational argument, and communication skills.

It should come as no surprise that one of Martin Luther's major challenges during the Protestant Reformation was to strip authority from the pope and place it in *sola scriptura*—Scripture alone. This doctrine, along with the idea of the priesthood of all believers, was unthinkable and impractical in the medieval world prior to the printing press. But this theology spread as a direct result of people having access to the Bible for themselves. It enabled the church to retrieve certain egalitarian aspects of authority found in the first-century church.

The printing press did not reverse the clock entirely. It didn't put information in the hands of everyone. Access to Scripture still required years of learning to decode the printed words. High-level reasoning and logic were required to sort out meanings. Because it took time and study to master these skills, authority remained primarily in the hands of scholars and pastors. However, they were no longer nearly as elite as the medieval scribes had been.

If the age of print introduced cracks in the information dam that separated priests from the people, then the electronic age detonated the dam, obliterating nearly all information barriers. The process of information becoming uncontrollable, which began with the telegraph, finds its fullest expression to date in the Internet. Along the way, radio and TV did their part to dismantle authority (whether parental, political, or religious).

Unlike the printed book or typed telegraph message, radio and TV have no "access codes." Reading and writing demand knowledge of an abstract system of meaningless shapes that need to be internalized in order to access information. No such skill is required to access the information being disseminated on radio or TV. These media forms communicate everything to everyone. As Neil Postman notes, "No child or adult becomes better at watching television by doing more of it. What skills are required are so elemental that we have yet to hear of a television viewing disability."[5] This means even very young children have access to the same information that adults have, undermining the monopolies of information.

This equal access to information leads to a diffusion of power and authority. We begin to believe there is no center (authority) or margin (follower) in the electronic world—everyone is a leader and everyone is a follower. As in oral cultures, in the electronic age authority tends to be communal and shared.

This is one reason why the emerging church is experimenting with new forms of preaching. Instead of a 30-minute monologue explaining a text from the Scriptures or a high-energy motivational guru offering fill-in-the-blank self-help tips from Jesus, emerging churches are experimenting with dialogue, shared storytelling, and picture shows in place of traditional sermons. This trend is partly the result of diminished attention spans thanks to our visual media and MTV hypercut editing, but it also has a great deal to do with the questioning and challenge to authority in the electronic age. In many emerging churches the pulpit is no longer the only seat for authority. Power is now dispersed among the pews.

A NEW VIEW OF LEADERSHIP

This shift toward information diffusion and the subsequent diffusion of power are providing us with a helpful corrective to the long history of centralized, top-down authority in the church. Electronic media allow us to retrieve the more participatory and egalitarian forms of leadership where authority is dynamic and based on relationships rather than on fixed job descriptions.

In this sense, electronic media help us revive the biblical vision in which authority and leadership are based not on exclusive access to information, but on personal character, spiritual vitality, gifts, and communal affirmation (Acts 15; 1 Corinthians 14; 1 Timothy 3:1-13; 5:17). Authority is still granted and leadership is still important, but seminary training and ordination are no longer the primary litmus tests of qualifying a person for leadership and authority.

The Pentecostal and Anabaptist traditions have long understood and applied this. Pentecostals historically located authority in a person's encounter with the Spirit. Anabaptists rotated the role of pastor throughout the church community on an annual basis to prevent power and pride from taking root. Over time, both of these traditions have taken more moderate positions on leadership, but their basic outlook is now making inroads among emerging churches.

While this move toward egalitarian leadership is positive in many ways, not everything is rosy: the effects of electronic media on church leadership can also lead to unintended negative consequences. These negative effects are often below our radar because they happen in slow and subtle ways.

The real loss for church leadership comes not from access to information, but rather from the form this readily available information is taking. We know the Graphic and Electronic Revolutions have undermined our capacity for the kind of high-level reasoning and abstract thought fostered during the print age. Electronic media encourage more right-brained, metaphorical modes of thinking and in turn atrophy left-brain, analytic capacities.

We have already looked at some of the cultural effects of this shift, but it presents a particular danger for the church. The impact of electronic media can cause us to lose touch with a crucial source of authority for our faith—the printed medium of Scripture. Along with the church, Scripture is God's other chosen medium for revelation and sending the gospel to the world. The vitality and faithfulness of the church depends upon our understanding of a printed medium. Consequently, leaders in the church need to have the left-brain capacities necessary to access this authority.

LOSING TOUCH WITH SCRIPTURE

The print age fostered the left brain muscles of critical reasoning, logic, and abstract thinking. The rules of logic that govern the printed word are neither intuitive nor innate to us; they require learning. It takes years to build up the intellectual capacity and patience necessary to understand arguments, unpack rhetoric, test "truth claims," debate meanings, and refute or appreciate conclusions. This is heavy lifting, and it requires no less lengthy or rigorous training than a weightlifter working to develop physical muscles. These capacities require mentoring, discipline, and extensive practice. In contrast, electronic media with their images and acoustic information require no time, skill, or energy to comprehend. The images entertain us and return us to the intuitive, right brain world of an oral culture.

In a very basic sense this return to right brain thinking undermines critical capacities for theological discernment and the faithful interpretation of Scripture. We need the rational left brain skills to develop coherence and discern meaning in our amorphous culture. Understanding Scripture, a printed medium, requires a capacity for reason and abstract thinking as well as the use of right brain impressions and intuitions. I'm not suggesting a return to modernity's tyranny of rationality and reason but inviting us to consider the immense value of such capacities.

Some will argue that electronic media forms such as the Internet still depend upon literacy, thereby nurturing the skills necessary to help us access Scripture. It is true that literacy is required for the Internet; however, it is a different kind from that demanded by a book. A book presents an extensive, in-depth monologue or a thorough argument carefully crafted in linear, successive paragraphs and pages (left brain). In contrast the Internet presents a nonlinear web of interconnected pages and a vast mosaic of hyperlinks with absolutely no beginning, middle, or end (right brain). This is one reason why Internet blogs reduce our capacity for carefully sustained critical reasoning and increase our preference for holistic synthesis and dialogue.[6]

Moreover, research shows that Internet users prefer content comprised of images, sounds, and pithy sentences presented in bullet-point form rather than lengthy pages of in-depth description or analysis.[7] In other words, the Internet develops superficial, holistic thought patterns in place of deep-level, linear reasoning skills. Our electronic media simply do not reinforce linear modes of logic, which causes us to prefer intuition, dialogue, and interconnecting ideas. These modes of thinking are not invalid or useless; in fact, they are extremely important and quite valuable. However, on their own they are insufficient for helping us understand Scripture, a crucial ingredient for leading God's people in the electronic age.

Scripture contains ideas with meanings that can easily be obscured by 2,000 years of history, language barriers, and enormous cultural differences. The Bible comes to us from another time and place. Its ancient context is assumed by its authors and thus never explained. The fact that it isn't explained means that faithful interpretation of Scripture requires some knowledge of this ancient context. All of this demands more of the left brain capacities that are eroding under the formative powers of the electronic age.

As long as we practice a religion dependent on a book, people of faith need the left brain capacities and knowledge necessary for accessing and interpreting Scripture faithfully. Consequently, leadership and authority should not be based only upon spiritual giftedness, a willingness to serve, or acceptance by the congregation. It should also include a growing knowledge of the gospel. Whether this comes through seminary training or other means, effective congregational leadership demands this capacity. We cannot ignore our need for leaders who function in ways similar to ancient scribes—those who have a deep knowledge of our sacred texts and traditions.

But here's the rub. These people inevitably hold monopolies on knowledge. As a result, their presence can sometimes undermine our best efforts at collaborative and dynamic forms of authority and leadership. The challenge, then, is for these leaders to develop an awareness of their power and find meaningful ways to share their knowledge with the people of God. This means serving as guides while also joining the congregation as members of the learning community, a community that devotes time to the practice of corporate study and reflection together. The leaders who hold unique knowledge have a legitimate authority as part of their gift and service to the community, but their ultimate goal is to find ways in which others can share in this knowledge and ultimately this authority.

READY...FIRE...AIM!

A former seminary professor of mine often jokes about his experience in church leadership. When it came to making decisions as a church, he said it was a not a "ready, aim, fire!" experience; instead it often felt more like a "ready, aim...aim, aim...ready, aim...aim, aim...aim, fire!" For his congregation, pulling the trigger was a bit of a challenge; they preferred processing ideas to taking action. In contrast, much of my experience in the evangelical world has felt more like a "ready, fire, aim!" experience. In our enthusiasm to reach the world for Christ and our unquestioning adoption of pragmatic marketplace practices, we stop asking difficult questions and start doing ministry. Too often we fire without ever setting our aim.

This can happen in a number of seemingly innocuous ways. When we import prepackaged programs from "successful" megachurches around the country, we assume they have already done the aiming for us, and all we have to do is pull the trigger. The best-selling Christian books are often those that offer practical self-help tips and reduce the complex mysteries of life to a series of simple answers, acronyms, and steps. The pastoral leadership section of the average Christian bookstore overflows with practical how-to manuals derived from the business principles of corporate America. Such books offer windows into our culture's preferences, capacities, and sensibilities. We can tolerate abstraction as long as it is immediately applicable and relevant to our lives. This proclivity is derived in part from exhaustion and the daily demands of ministry. But it is also caused by the power of electronic media to atrophy our tolerance for complexity, nuance, and high degrees of abstraction.

Given this reality, the loss for the church and the challenge for leaders is a subtle one. Our culture's voracious appetite for practical application is displacing our capacity and concern for meaningful theological reflection and study. This is a lamentable reality for the church, because it means we set out with our hands tied as we navigate through rapid changes while faithfully trying to form God's people. The culture of unbridled pragmatism is our reality, and it calls for a respectful understanding of its limits. However, as leaders in the church we are invited to model another way.

RECOVERING THE RHYTHM OF "PRAXIS"

Freeing our hands will mean helping our communities move from clamoring for proven practices to recovering the ancient art of *praxis*. Praxis refers to a way of living in which our reflection and study are informed by our action and engagement, while our action and engagement are informed by our study. Figure 10 below diagrams the rhythm of praxis.

THE RHYTHM OF PRAXIS[8]

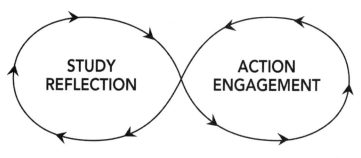

FIGURE 10

This is an ongoing cycle in which each activity informs the other. Our programs and practices should be informed by the truths gleaned from study and reflection. Likewise, our study and reflection should not simply be exercises in abstract thinking. They are to be intimately tied to, concerned with, and informed by the concrete practices in the life of the congregation. This is a fading art in many evangelical churches. With the consuming demands of ministry and congregations who have little interest in or time for the rigors of study, the vast majority of evangelicals find themselves caught in a never-ending circle of executing and maintaining programs. Our invitation in the evangelical world is to take time as congregations to loop back from our seasons of activity for seasons of reflection and study.

Our interest and ability to engage in praxis requires a reservoir of interpretive skills and a firm knowledge of Scripture. This means that people of faith need access to the ancient world, languages, and history of the church. Our leaders must learn and experiment with ways to connect the ancient horizon of the text with the contemporary horizon of our current context. This is not simply a question of application. This is about mutual interpretation.

Mutual interpretation moves us to ask different questions in our Bible studies. Instead of contemplating the question "How does this apply to my life?" we consider the question "What does this call us to?" In this sense we don't simply interpret the Bible; we allow the Bible to interpret us.[9] Neither do we simply study the Bible as an abstract artifact dispensing universal truths. Instead, we allow our personal and corporate hopes and hurts to be present in the conversation with Scripture.

This can be practiced in a variety of practical ways. I know several congregations who hold small gatherings with the pastor a week before the worship service to discuss the passage to be preached on the following week. The meetings are designed to let the members of the community encounter the text with their own experiences, questions, and observations. In the process, the hopes, pains, and fears of the people are given a chance to mingle with the text. The preacher may also share certain observations, musings, and relevant research. In the days following, the person who will be preaching retreats to study, reflect, and refine the sermon with the experiences and associations of the group in mind. This is a form of praxis. When the sermon is preached, it is a product of the community, the community's interaction with the text, and the preacher's expertise as a theologian in residence. Other congregations practice open feedback after a sermon, giving the congregation a chance to share their associations or encounters with the sermon or the text.

Praxis is by no means limited to issues of preaching and teaching. This rhythm of reflection and action, action and reflection, can be practiced in everything from the decisions about how we worship to setting our priorities for missional engagement to the development of community.

CREATING COLLABORATIVE AUTHORITY

Looking back, I have some regrets about the way I led as president of my fraternity. I chose to lead in a more top-down style in part because it mirrored the approach of most of the pastors I knew. These pastors had made the top-down model of leadership their default position. They were gifted leaders and knew different styles were needed for different settings, but they generally operated from more authoritarian stances.

As we consider the postmodern situation and revisit the biblical witness, I believe a more faithful and relevant approach is to invert this pattern, making collaborative and egalitarian structures our default with a limited use of top-down authority.

We learn in Paul's letters to Timothy that there are clear leadership roles in the church (1 Timothy 3:1-13; 5:17). However, in his references to bishops, deacons, and elders, Paul does not tell of an established hierarchy for these roles. It is clear these roles have authority, but Paul is not concerned with telling us who is "above" whom. Too often we read our modern definitions of these words back into Paul's writings. While there is no single leadership structure put forth by the New Testament, there is strong support for more collaborative models (Acts 15; 1 Corinthians 14:23-27).

As authority is diffused throughout the congregation and as the emerging church seeks to develop collaborative leadership styles that affirm the gifts of the body and the priesthood of all believers, there are practical questions to be considered. If everyone has authority on some level, how do decisions get made? And who has the power and authority to make them? There are no simple answers to these questions. However, I have experienced one approach that is surprisingly effective and especially appropriate for our electronic culture with its heightened suspicion of authority.

During my seminary years my wife, Andrea, and I were very involved in an urban Anabaptist congregation with a theology strongly rooted in postmodern sensibilities. We learned quickly that this congregation used a strange method for making major decisions in the church—they didn't vote in a democratic fashion where the majority rules. Instead they required a consensus.

Initially, I thought this was crazy. How can you get 150 people in a room with all their diverse personalities, pathologies, and opinions and ever hope to achieve consensus in this lifetime? I talked about this method with Jim Brenneman, our lead pastor. He explained that such a process takes more time and more conversation to achieve, but it builds remarkable unity. In addition, when you use consensus, there is no such thing as a minority in the congregation—everyone has a voice. This may sound risky, but it is less so than one might think.

The effect is a paradoxical one. Each person in the room is given full power and authority to stop a decision or action being taken by the congregation. Because everyone in the room has all the power, no one is jockeying for the power—they already have it. In an unexpected way this nurtures caution and humility in people. It minimizes hidden agendas and breeds a deep commitment to unity. As people are invited to listen to the Holy Spirit and given the freedom to voice concerns, disagreements, wonderings, and joys, the process becomes less threatening. The tone of such meetings is often hopeful and expectant even in the midst of vigorous debate or disagreement.

A few years ago our church was in a process of discerning whether or not to move our worship service from Sunday evening at 6 p.m. to Sunday morning at 9 a.m. Such a decision would only be made if there was consensus by the entire congregation (again, it sounded crazy). We held a number of meetings complete with heated debate, disagreement, and strongly opposing views. The opposing views were not just rooted in personal or practical preferences. For some in the congregation there were even theological principles at stake. Over time a majority of the congregation got behind the decision to hold the service in the morning. However, eight members who disagreed with the decision held out and wanted further discussion before a decision was made.

We had one final meeting in an effort to make a decision. The dissenting members came before the congregation and said, "We strongly disagree with this decision, but we are willing to go with the rest of the congregation." They decided to lay their agendas and preferences aside for the sake of congregational unity. The next Sunday morning all of the dissenting members showed up at the service in their pajamas.

This playful protest broke the tension, instilled laughter, and re-affirmed their solidarity with the rest of the congregation. They were numerically a minority, but they had been granted full power and authority to stop a decision. In this moment they were important leaders in the congregation even though they did not hold official positions.

In a democratic setting where the majority rules by 51 percent, there is always a minority group left without power who can easily feel marginalized. This can breed power struggles where the minority seeks to undermine and disrupt the decision even after it has been made. Ruling by majority is typically a more efficient method than consensus, but it has a tendency to amplify divisions and differences.

CONSENSUS AS A MISSIONAL PRACTICE

It is important to note that a healthy practice of consensus depends upon strong leadership and an ability to instill in members a deep commitment to the greater good of the community. Our pastor admits that when he first started using consensus decision-making practices 18 years ago, he was terrified. His decision to do it was based not on the practical benefits noted above, as he discovered those only later. Instead his conviction came from the belief that the church was to be a sign of God's kingdom, always witnessing to the unique nature of that kingdom, where those who seek to be first will be last and those who seek to lose their lives will gain them.

Jesus did not seek to establish a grand hierarchy of leadership. Instead he modeled service and humility by washing the disciples' feet. We learn in Acts 15:28-29 that the early church made certain decisions by unanimous consent, not by authoritarian decree. These were missional practices that went against the common sense of the day and affirmed God's preference for inverting power structures and speaking truth through minority voices like those of outsiders—a humble carpenter, and uneducated fishermen.

In many ways, postmodern culture encourages a recovery of egalitarian modes of authority and leadership. Electronic culture prompts us to reconsider collaborative, team-based leadership in which we are keenly aware that Christ, not the pastor, is the head of the body (Ephesians 4:15). Consensus decision-making helps us do this. It is an immensely underutilized resource for building unity and witnessing to the upside-down kingdom of God. This is foreign territory for most of us, and it may not be the best approach in every situation, but it is worth looking at some of its practical mechanics.

The Practical Side of Consensus

No single style of decision-making will be right for every situation. In an effort to help you determine whether this form of decision-making is right for your context, I have included the steps used by our Mennonite church to facilitate a consensus process for making major decisions.

GUIDELINES FOR CONSENSUS DECISION MAKING

Adapted from Pasadena Mennonite Church[10]

The ultimate goal in the consensus process is to make discerning judgments that are faithful to the Holy Spirit and Scripture. The process calls for an awareness of the precious value of both people and time. The intention is that issues are fully aired, participants are given a voice and listened to, and no individual or subgroup influences the group unduly. The consensus process requires participants to be emotionally present and engaged, frank in a loving and respectful manner, and sensitive to each other, and to discipline personal passions and views for the sake of inclusive conversation.

It should be noted that anyone is welcome to be part of the conversation, but only members of the church may cast their votes. What follows is a set of guidelines for consensus decision-making at Pasadena Mennonite Church.

I. SETTING THE TONE

The moderator invites the group to ready itself for yielding to the Holy Spirit and to each other. Vulnerability and openness to joy, pain, the unknown, and the unexpected are encouraged. The spirit of the meeting should ensure participants that they are in a safe place where they may speak freely and receive and give love, grace, and forgiveness. A period of silence, a spoken prayer, or a meditation can be helpful in developing the group's sense of discernment.

II. PREPARING FOR GROUP DISCUSSION

At the meeting the moderator presents the agenda, including

1. Clearly stated topic(s) for discussion
2. The action for each topic (i.e., a discussion or a decision)
3. The estimated time needed for each topic

III. GROUP DISCUSSION

A. Following the introduction of the topic, anyone may respond with an idea for discussion. This may be an opinion, a further definition of the problem, a suggested approach to the issue, or a proposal for a decision.

B. The moderator is primarily responsible for

1. Keeping the discussion focused on the topic
2. Providing clarification or rephrasing as needed
3. Summarizing underlying agreements and differences
4. Identifying new issues as they arise
5. Ensuring that all viewpoints are heard and understood by the group.
6. Identifying problems with the group process and seeking to remedy them

C. If the tenor of the discussion becomes unruly, unfocused, or otherwise undesirable, the moderator may suggest a period of silence and recentering and clarify possible options for continuing the process.

D. After most viewpoints have been expressed and/or some part of the discussion begins to be repeated, the moderator states the conclusion toward which the members appear to be moving. At this point, it is essential that objections and ambivalence be heard.

IV. MAKING THE DECISION

A. The moderator states the perceived direction and asks the members if there are final objections or if consensus has been reached.

B. Final concerns are discussed, and the process of developing agreement continues until a decision is endorsed by the whole group. Final endorsement occurs when the moderator reviews the decision and there are no further objections or suggested changes by the members.

V. IF THE GROUP CANNOT AGREE

A. The group may not have enough information to make a good decision. A decision may need to be deferred until more facts can be gathered and/or people have more time for prayer and reflection.

B. Disagreement and dissent: Consensus does not imply unanimous enthusiasm for a decision. Rather one must be able to live with, support, and commit oneself to not undermining the decision. When the process has fully run its course and an individual does not agree with the decision being endorsed by the group, there are two possible responses:

1. Standing aside: The member disagrees but will not prevent the group from endorsing a decision.
2. Principled objection: The dissenting member states that passage of the decision would be a violation of deeply held values and convictions and asks the group not to endorse the decision. In such instances, the action or decision is not taken. The dissenting member may offer another solution for discussion, request more time for study and reflection, or simply hold to the objection.

VII. PROXY AND PRESENCE

By definition the consensus process assumes that people are present at the meeting; thus, the concept of proxy is not applicable to this model. People who cannot attend a scheduled meeting or those who must leave early should not expect to convey sentiment for the group to consider in their absence.

A PLACE FOR CENTRALIZED AUTHORITY

Consensus is just one approach to making decisions, but it is not intended as a model for making every decision in a church. It can be extremely effective when it comes to major congregational issues; however, when dealing with the decisions of day-to-day ministry, consensus can become both cumbersome and counterproductive. In certain situations authority needs to be centralized and leaders must be granted the power to make decisions without consulting anyone.

This particular authority is granted by virtue of a leader's sacrifice and service to the community. Without this authority, leaders in the congregation tend to burn out quickly. I have seen the most burnout in settings where lay leaders do a great deal of work but have very little authority to make decisions on their own. The most effective solution has often been corporately and publicly to grant leaders the authority they need to accomplish their tasks. More often than not the burden of their service to the community is greatly eased by this simple act.

This occurred most dramatically in our congregation when we moved from an egalitarian process of planning worship to a more centralized model. Initially, our worship services were planned by a group of laypeople who were responsible for different aspects of the service but had equal say in the other elements of the service. While the structure was intended to encourage greater involvement by the congregation, it actually led to a talent drain as people slowly began to resign from the worship team. Increasingly, people became exhausted by the frequent second-guessing by other members of the group. Over time the worship services took on a disjointed and lethargic quality.

As frustration mounted, we created a worship discernment team to pause and revisit our theology of worship and our current structures. It was clear to us that our church placed a high premium on congregational involvement but that the current structures were encouraging less involvement. Our solution was to develop a more centralized, authoritative structure that balanced the need for contribution from the congregation. We recruited and organized four worship teams, each with two leaders. The teams would rotate every week. One leader was responsible for planning and leading all the musical elements in the service, while the other leader was charged with planning all the other elements of the service (i.e., flow, communion, liturgy, art, dance, etc.). They would meet to plan together, but each was given full autonomy and authority to implement whatever he or she chose, no questions asked.

It started as an experiment, but it worked better than we expected. The result for the leaders was a new sense of freedom and a greater feeling of being appreciated for their ministry. It instilled a degree of confidence in them that was quickly passed on to their team members and eventually led to greater vitality, consistency, and energy in the worship service. It did not fix all of our problems, but the shift toward more centralized leadership actually encouraged greater lay involvement.

NAVIGATING THE KNIFE'S EDGE

We walk a fine line. Electronic culture is helping us recover a biblical vision for more collaborative and egalitarian leadership models. This can be meaningfully practiced in a number of ways. Specific resources, such as consensus decision-making, resonate with emerging culture and become missional activities that bear witness to the nature of God's kingdom.

Electronic culture is also presenting critical challenges. Authority for our faith is still based on an ancient book whose meanings are made murkier by the legacy of electronic media. Electronic culture, with its right brain bias and overwhelming options for easy entertainment, is undermining our interest in and capacity for accessing a critical source of authority—Scripture. Our great challenge as leaders is to engage ourselves and our congregations in the art of *praxis* as an invaluable means of stitching together our calling to be faithful interpreters of the gospel and our calling to be engaged in our culture.

WORSHIP IN ELECTRONIC CULTURE

CHAPTER EIGHT

The room is dimly lit by the glimmer of candles. The smell of coffee permeates the air, inadvertently serving as sacred incense. Chairs and couches are informally arranged in a circle. There is no clear center or margin to the room; there is no stage. Off to one side, hidden in shadows, a band leads worship songs while some congregants informally play along with percussion instruments. Projected on a wall are looping silent video clips interspersing images of faith and culture—a potter's hands molding clay, a snowboarder catching air, clenched hands draped with prayer beads, a snapshot of '80s-style break-dancers, and so on. In one corner people are arranged on prayer kneelers, anointing each other with oil. In another corner people are serving each other bread and wine in hushed voices. In another corner people are spread out on the floor painting, drawing, or sculpting with clay. Between songs the pastor periodically shares

"THE NEW PREFERENCE FOR DEPTH PARTICIPATION HAS PROMPTED IN THE YOUNG A STRONG DRIVE TOWARDS RELIGIOUS EXPERIENCE WITH RICH LITURGICAL OVERTONES. THE LITURGICAL REVIVAL OF THE ELECTRONIC AGE AFFECTS EVEN THE MOST AUSTERE PROTESTANT SECTS."[1]

—MARSHALL MCLUHAN, 1964

a Bible verse and a few brief thoughts, eliciting dialogue and feedback but being careful not to exude an aura of too much authority. Some participants sit listening while others pray in their corners or periodically migrate from one station to the next.

If you have never experienced an emerging worship gathering, this is a glimpse of what you might find. While there is no rule book or universal model, the scene above reflects many of the aesthetic sensibilities of emerging worship gatherings. Experiential participation is the main emphasis in such a gathering. And once again, the quotation at the head of the chapter reveals that McLuhan anticipated this kind of liturgical revival in the church decades before it occurred.

The Electronic Age has led to these emerging worship gatherings, which have both inspired hope and incited controversy from different corners of the church. In one corner some large conservative evangelical churches claim these new forms of worship are compromising the gospel truths and traditions, eroding sound teaching, and leading people to the insidious moral relativism of postmodern culture. In another corner the radical innovators allege emerging churches aren't going far enough. These innovators fear many churches are merely developing superficial "emerging worship services" without paying serious attention to very real changes in the emerging theology of church.

Worship styles and services are notoriously polarizing forces in the church. Emerging worship gatherings are no exception. In this chapter we will see the implications of McLuhan's perspective when it comes to worship. To do so, we need to get the lay of the land to see what's happening.

THE MAC VERSUS WINDOWS APPROACH

In the early days of the personal computing revolution, one operating system became an industry standard. Manufactured by Microsoft, the disk operating system (DOS) relied on keyboard commands and computer language for navigating the system. It was laborious and took time to learn but eventually became efficient for those who mastered it.

Then one day Steve Jobs, founder of Apple Computers, developed a completely different operating system from the ground up.

It was called the Macintosh OS and was designed entirely around a graphical user interface (GUI). This was a different kind of operating system that presented users with a virtual desktop featuring intuitive icons and visual folders that could be manipulated and moved with a mouse rather than with cumbersome keyboard commands. Sales took off as consumers discovered it was a far more user-friendly way to do personal computing.

As Microsoft's sales began to slow, it launched a new operating system known as Windows. It was still based on the cumbersome DOS system, but it featured a cosmetic layer that looked almost identical to the graphical Mac OS. While these systems looked similar, they were built in completely different ways and operated with totally different assumptions.

The story of computer operating systems is an appropriate metaphor for what has been happening in the emerging church. In the most basic sense some churches are responding to emerging culture by doing what Mac did—innovating from the inside out—whereas others are opting for the Windows approach to the emerging church—making cosmetic changes but keeping the same foundation.

Those who prefer the "Mac approach" are innovators and church planters who start with a postmodern theology of church and allow their forms to mirror their theologies—in other words, the methods and the message change. This is a ground-up, inside-out approach. Many of these church leaders have grown dissatisfied with the mark modernity has left on the church. They recognize that modern Protestants have an impoverished theology of the church, the result of being reared in a faith that emphasizes individualism and reinforces consumerism. In addition, they believe modern Christians have become too concerned with defending a rational, propositional, and private faith while ignoring the power and importance of story, experience, and the call to community. Innovators of the emerging church fear that the modern church is more concerned with growth derived from meeting marketplace demands than nurturing missional communities.

As a result these "Mac" innovators have begun rethinking church. They are not simply concerned with reaching an underserved "target market"; they want a revolution of the people of God. They have been nurturing small organic communities formed by postmodern theological sensibilities, and they are seeking to restore an appreciation for narrative, the value of experience, and the role of the kingdom of God in the gospel. While these characteristics have echoes of Protestant liberalism, the innovators have held firmly to the authority of Scripture and the imperative of the Great Commission. These communities have been experimenting with alternative forms of worship to reflect their theologies and resonate with the emerging generation.

The "Windows" approach is well-represented by several of the "celebrity" pastors in the megachurch movement who are strong advocates of the emerging church. They defend emerging worship services not simply as okay but as imperative for reaching the next generation. Their basic argument is rooted in the familiar belief that as long as our message stays the same, our methods can and should change.[2]

As large evangelical churches began to see the slow but real migration of the younger generation away from church or to smaller emerging churches, they did what Microsoft did. They began to mirror the aesthetics of these "Mac" communities by developing alternative worship services targeting the emerging generation. Motivated by a deep evangelistic longing to reach a "lost" generation, their new services adopted many of the forms frequently employed in emerging churches. This cosmetic alteration ensured that they were competitive and fashionable. However, they remained committed to the theological assumptions of modernity. These new cosmetics have had the effect of drawing hundreds, even thousands of people from the emerging generation, but deliberately little has been done to address the limits of a modern conception of the gospel message, in part because it is assumed to be *the* unchanging version.

THE LURE OF SPECTACLE

The "Mac" crowd represents a minority in the emerging church and has at times expressed frustration with the more dominant "Windows" approach. They fear that while these aesthetic changes are extremely attractive to a postmodern generation, they are little more than surface fixes that miss the point. They find that these large-scale "experiential/emerging/alternative" worship services are executed with excellence and give people an experience of God but are doing little to challenge the individualistic, consumer-driven approach to faith. The Mac-style leaders in the emerging church are less interested in making aesthetic changes and more concerned with rescuing the church from the theological compromise brought about by modernity and the contamination of the consumer marketplace.

The critique by "Mac" innovators is a fair one. As noted in Chapter Five, the modern church, despite its best efforts, has unintentionally fallen into many of the traps that result from trying to compete in the consumer marketplace. In reality, the modern church gained tremendous momentum in the '80s and '90s by responding to the consumer demand for spectacle. People in our culture are drawn and stirred into frenzy by large-scale events such as rock concerts, sporting events, or celebrity awards shows. Imitating these spectacles, the modern church learned that if you put on a great show with a talented, high-energy motivational speaker and an outstanding band playing compelling music, people will come.

On the surface, the "Windows" approach to an emerging worship service appears very different from these spectacular and highly polished contemporary services targeting boomers. This is in part because emerging culture has a high degree of cynicism and tends to be very suspicious of manipulation. As a result, it tends to eschew packaged and polished services. In response, Windows-style leaders developed a different cosmetic layer that appears raw, organic, and unpolished. These "alternative" worship services seek to invite a climate of experiential participation instead of passive observation. However, this does not mean they are immune to becoming consumer-driven spectacles. Behind these new services is the same basic modern belief that effective evangelism requires an imitative response to consumer demands in our culture. At the end of the day this is still target marketing, not church.

THE CREATION OF INSUFFICIENT COMMUNITY

Spectacle is not an entirely bad thing; there are clearly elements of worship that call for excellence and are rooted in performance, drama, and reenactment. However, left unchecked, spectacles actually work against the creation of authentic, missional community. Spectacle creates publics, not communities.[3]

Publics are made up of people who share the same affinities but are otherwise leading disparate lives. A spectacle invites as many people as possible to come and have personal encounters. In the case of a worship service, the gathered crowd may share an affinity for musical styles, a particular preacher, or a personal experience of God. The church is about the big weekend encounter, but once people have had their encounters, everyone goes their separate ways. Their worship experience has little to do with sharing life together and nothing to do with a corporate mission in the world. It is about personal transformation and private faith.

In this sense, spectacle—by its very nature—reinforces an individualistic understanding of faith. As a result, leaders in such churches spend extensive amounts of time and resources seeking ways to encourage and channel people into small groups in a noble effort to build community. Those responsible for doing this can attest that this is a bit like trying to build community among strangers at an airport waiting for the same plane. Unfortunately, the weekend attractions that are so successful in drawing crowds comprise the very force that works against the creation of missional community.

I want to be clear on this point: personal transformation and an experience of God are not invalid. Neither is enjoying music or being moved by a talented speaker. These are wonderful gifts, and the modern evangelical church has achieved these things with remarkable skill. The point is not that they are invalid; rather, they are insufficient. In this way, the modern approach to church has given us a legacy of personal transformation but has truncated the true height, length, depth, and breadth of the gospel that calls us to become the corporate body of Christ—a missional community, God's chosen medium to represent the kingdom on earth, bring healing, confront injustice, wage peace, and participate in the ministry of reconciliation modeled by the way of Jesus.

VIDEO VENUES: THE SPECTACLE OF CELEBRITY

One of the increasingly popular initiatives in the "Windows" camp of the emerging church is the use of multisite, video-venue worship services. This is a model wherein multiple congregations are sprinkled throughout a city or campus, but one preacher is piped in to each gathering via a live video feed. This is an attempt to retain continuity of message while still attracting congregants by letting them participate in ways that are more convenient or that suit their personal preferences. Its proponents argue that such a method offers the best of both worlds: you don't have to commute; you get to worship your way; and you don't have to sacrifice great preaching.

I visited a church recently on the day it was launching its multisite service. I watched the sermon live, while two other gatherings in other parts of the city watched via large projection screens. It was a stellar sermon by an extraordinarily gifted preacher well known in Christian subculture. But the most striking feature of the sermon was that his message was being directly contradicted by his medium—the video venue.

Here's how. The pastor was speaking on the difference between talent and character and how too often we emphasize talent in ministry more than character. He began with an object lesson. There on stage next to him was a huge dictionary set on a high stool. As he spoke, he began to dispense several cans of whipped cream on top of the dictionary, creating a white, fluffy mound. When he finished, he told us that the dictionary was our character, the firm foundation. The whipped cream was our talent, something very attractive but lacking substance. After this setup he concluded by saying, "If your ministry is based on character, it will last, but if your ministry is based on talent..." He paused and then swatted the mound of whipped cream. In one swoop it was all over the floor, and he continued, "...your ministry will suffer when times get tough."

His message was excellent and told an important truth—ministry is supported by character, not talent. However, the medium of the video venue had a subliminal message of its own. The message of a video-venue sermon is that the authority to preach is derived from talent and celebrity, not character or communal affirmation. A televised event doesn't communicate anything about a person's character. It can only affirm or deny talent and attractiveness. We don't watch movies or TV shows because we respect or want to know the personal characters of the actors. We watch because we are enamored by their beauty, talent, or celebrity.

Character is known only through communal affirmation, which requires some personal knowledge of one another. This personal knowledge is impossible for satellite congregations who only see the pastor's performance. The congregation witnessing a sermon via video can only assess whether the preacher is talented, not whether she has character.

Not only did the medium itself undermine this particular preacher's message, but the extensive financial outlay required to pull off a video-venue service also communicated to the congregation that only a preacher with a golden tongue has authority to preach the gospel. It conveys the unspoken belief that no one in the satellite congregation has the authority to speak to their context because preaching requires unique talents that only a few actually possess. Like the wizard in *The Wizard of Oz,* only the larger-than-life giants, painted by pixelated light and hovering above the congregation, possess these elusive talents. The medium itself nurtures an elite priestly class in which the preacher is set apart from the people. With video venues we can say goodbye to the priesthood of all believers and hello to the papacy of celebrity.

Even if this attitude is explicitly denied by the preacher, the very medium reinforces the belief that only talented people with some degree of celebrity can or should preach. Even if laypeople were encouraged to share a word from God before the church, the pressure would be too much for most of us. Few people possess the confidence and charisma to preach before thousands, let alone before the unflinching gaze of the camera vicariously channeling the eyes of others who witness and study every amplified movement or mistake.

My critique of this situation has nothing to do with the preacher's theology, character, or intention. In fact, I have great respect and admiration for this person. The problem comes from a lack of awareness for how media shapes our message in worship. When we ignore the power of media, its effects often go undetected. As a result, we fail to perceive the unintended consequences of our decisions and the ways our media undermine our message.

ACCIDENTAL CHANGES IN OUR THINKING

My critique of Windows-style worship is not intended as a wholesale dismissal of the blood, sweat, and tears shed by faithful Christian leaders. My goal is not to invalidate their approach to ministry. Instead my intent is to help us anticipate the unintended consequences that result from the way we do worship. As long as our worship forms are designed in response to meeting perceived needs and consumer demands, we will continue to reinforce a consumer gospel of individualism and dissolve our theology of church. Our message will reflect our medium.

At the same time because our medium is our message, there is a strange phenomenon occurring in these Windows-based emerging churches. Many of them are accidentally discovering and preferring more postmodern ways of thinking. Because the medium is the message, the very forms of emerging worship actually undermine modern approaches to theology. Like all media, emerging worship practices are not merely imitative, they are also generative—they shape us. The reality is that as our forms change, so does our thinking. In this sense, despite these churches' best intentions to retain the same message, these new worship forms actually nurture certain aspects of postmodern thinking.

Whether our approach is "Mac" or "Windows," emerging worship gatherings create a right brain experience of God. This happens when we throw out linear rows of pews in favor of nonlinear clusters of couches or displace the centrality of the preaching event with experiential rituals. As Chapter Four illustrated, the image-based, experiential aspects of worship develop more right brain thought patterns. This has a tendency to erode the left brain preference for understanding rational propositions as the primary means to gaining faith or growing in Christ. Instead, these forms develop a new appreciation for mystery, experience, and intuition as central elements of faith. In this way, emerging forms of worship are creating more Eastern and medieval approaches to church and theology.

Even the simple shift of focusing on participation over performance inevitably leads to a decentralized attitude toward leadership and authority, because each person assumes an active role in worship rather than passively observing the role of the pastor. All of these forms plant the seeds for postmodern thinking and perceiving.

THE ILLUSION OF RELEVANCE

Relevance is a buzzword in the church. It became increasingly popular during the age of modernity when the church was slowly pushed from the center of society to the margins. From the sidelines, the church was forced to discover meaningful contact points with culture in order remain vital. The liberal church adopted humanism and assumed the role of a chaplain to society for civil functions. Conservative evangelicals became players in the consumer marketplace by concerning themselves with conversion in the private lives of individuals. In the postmodern age, we are beginning to see the limits of these options.

We have seen there is no longer a belief in a grand, unifying metanarrative that occupies the center in our culture. This is one reason McLuhan used the metaphor of "acoustic space" to describe the Electronic Age. In the world of acoustic space there is no center or margin. It is "boundless, directionless, horizonless."[5] In such a setting the church exists amid the swirling sea of pluralism and complexity. [6] As a result, relevance is a moving target that has never been more difficult or confusing to achieve. The strain from these demands is beginning to show; depression and health problems are on the rise among pastors. According to one survey, the number one reason pastors leave the church is feeling inadequate to manage the complexities of the job.[7]

In the midst of this, a flood of books and conferences urges pastors to find ways to become relevant to culture. This usually means the adoption of multimedia technology and hardware as a central part of worship. Their logic is simple: "The language of the culture is electronic media; therefore, we should speak that language in the church."

Many in the church are responding to this by taking risks with electronic media. Extensive resources are being sunk into editing equipment, audio systems, video projectors, light shows, and more. There is no other period in church history when relevance has cost so much time and money. And this kind of technology is only getting more expensive. Most congregations simply cannot afford these things, but they are encouraged to seek them as means to an evangelistic end.

While the impetus to speak the language of the culture and respond to the postmodern shift is crucial, the champions of electronic relevance bind another oppressive yoke to the already-bent backs of pastors in our culture. Relevance does not come simply from imitating culture or mirroring the techniques of Hollywood and Madison Avenue. It does not depend upon the adoption of electronic hardware in worship. Relevance is derived from experimenting with authentic and indigenous practices that emerge from the gift mix of a particular congregation for a local community.

The vast majority of congregations will never come close to competing with Hollywood when it comes to electronic entertainment. Consider our cultural diet of advertising alone. We consume thousands of 30-second TV ads each week. These invasive parables of corporate branding permeate our lives, cost millions of dollars, and take months of planning to produce. This is the steady media diet to which we have grown accustomed (to say nothing of the film and TV industry). Compare this with the resources of local congregations. If our worship services imitate these forms with amateur multimedia slide shows and homemade videos in an effort to be relevant, it's like serving Ramen noodles to people who eat catered meals every day. Our approach simply cannot be one of cultural imitation.

This does not mean electronic media belong only in the hands of experts. Rather, this is an invitation to pause and reflect on the passions and gifts of our congregations. It is an opportunity to ask pointed questions about our use of electronic media. Are our practices indigenous or imitative? Do they emanate from the artistic impetus of the Spirit or a response to consumer demands? These are the subtle but crucial assessments we must make when determining why and how to employ electronic media in worship.

WORSHIP WITHOUT HARDWARE

It should be clear by now that I am not opposed to electronic multimedia in worship. I think they are entirely appropriate when they are innate to our congregational gift mix and when there is an awareness of the power of such media to shape a message. One church I visited has a number of members from the entertainment industry—artists, writers, directors, actors, and editors. On numerous occasions they have written, shot, and produced several videos and short films for worship that worked remarkably well for conveying certain aspects of the gospel. In this context the extensive use of electronic media reflected and respected the unique gifting of their community.

While this is positive, the congregation has taken little time to consider the unintended effects of their media. An extensive use of video clips and short films in worship turns the congregation into an audience expecting to be entertained. When electronic media are taken to extremes, we become spectators of the gospel rather than participants in the kingdom of God.

For the rest of us who find ourselves in congregational settings with tight budgets or limited talent in the area of electronic media, our invitation is to develop our own indigenous practices that connect with our electronic culture. This does not mean we have to be completely original; there is much we can retrieve from history, tradition, and other congregations. More importantly, we must recognize that using electronic media is not the only way to become relevant in our culture.

The congregation I've been worshiping with for the past several years has very limited resources. We don't even use a projection screen. Nonetheless, we still speak the language of electronic culture in other ways. As already discussed, electronic culture is an increasingly right brain world. It is this underlying attribute to which our church seeks to respond. As a result we work to incorporate more right brain practices rooted in experiential participation that are borrowed from medieval Catholic spirituality and Eastern Orthodox worship, neither of which demands electronic media.

For example, we participate in the experiential ritual of communion in ways that emphasize an intimate community meal. We allow both pastors and laypeople to serve the meal. When congregants come forward, groups of eight to ten form a circle around the table and are served together. When one group is finished, the next group comes forward. It is a small gesture, but it emphasizes the corporate and participatory nature of the ritual.

In other parts of the service, we invite small but significant body movements and prayer postures as part of our liturgy. We invite members of the congregation to create and share art installations such as paintings, sculpture, or interactive stations to be used for different seasons of the church calendar.

During one particular Good Friday service, a member prepared an interactive sculpture for part of worship. She used a dead tree branch to create a small tree. On the twigs and branches she'd hooked hundreds of leaves cut from brown construction paper. Each leaf had a word like *grief, envy, bitterness,* or *doubt* written on it. Strewn beneath the tree were similar leaves made from green paper. They were all blank. We were invited to remove a brown leaf of our choosing; write a new word, such as *hope, joy, reconciliation,* or *peace* on a green leaf; and affix it to the tree. It was a powerful, participatory, and corporate sculpture that invited a more right brain encounter with God and one another. This is just one example of the many authentic and relevant expressions of worship in electronic culture that doesn't use extensive multimedia hardware. My hope is that we consider creative ways to encounter our media culture without fueling the appetite for more and better electronic hardware.

THE INEVITABILITY OF IRRELEVANCE

The danger in pursuing the holy grail of relevance is that we become chameleons, morphing into whatever colors our culture puts before us. We run the risk of inadvertently camouflaging the very aspects of the gospel that should remain visible. Relevance taken to an extreme serves to put our lamp under a bowl. In the process we lose our distinctive identity as a penetrating contrast society in the world. If we are truly faithful to the gospel and authentic in our identity as the people of God, we will inevitably betray aspects of cultural *irrelevance*.

In this way, the incarnation is the most helpful guide for engaging culture. The incarnation of Jesus shows us an important truth. Jesus came into the world speaking the language, living the customs, and using the forms meaningful for people living in a particular time and place. At the same time, Jesus challenged and inverted many of those same forms, customs, and symbols. He reinterpreted the Passover meal in light of his own death. He overturned the temple tables, healed on the Sabbath, and advocated nonviolent resistance. In many ways these acts were profoundly irrelevant and even dangerous in that culture; some of them still are today. These acts reflected values of the kingdom of God that radically countered those of broader culture.

Likewise, incarnational worship should give serious consideration to the context of the gathered community. This means working with the media, language, and symbols of a given context and discerning the ways these might be used in our corporate expressions of worship. If our worship is incarnational, we will reinterpret, challenge, and critique certain cultural forms and symbols. We may challenge our consumer tendencies, defend hope in a cynical age, or practice ancient rituals that affirm God's all-encompassing story in a culture that rejects metanarratives. Some of our worship practices and beliefs will seem foreign and strange to the world; yet it is this aspect of our worship that points to our distinct identity as the people of God, a people rooted in the values and vision of God's kingdom. Incarnational worship is authentic and culturally engaged, prophetic and pastoral, relevant and resistant. This way we remove our bowl and reflect the light of Christ in dark places.

COUNTERING CONSUMERISM

The emerging church has tapped into the experiential longing of a generation through the creation of worship that is nonlinear, holistic, multisensory, and participatory. The scene described at the beginning of this chapter offers an example of this. While I am an advocate for such experiments, there is—as always—an unintended consequence to this approach. One of the distinctive features of emerging worship services is the use of concurrent elements—several things happening at the same time. This offers a variety of ways for people to encounter God. You can paint, contemplate moving icons, take communion, kneel at prayer benches, listen to music, or join the pastor's conversation/sermon. Reflecting the sensibilities of our culture, this is a way of worship that allows for a self-directed and participatory encounter with God.

The emphasis here is not simply on experience but also on personal preference. The subtle message of using concurrent elements is, "You are an individual, a consumer. Do whatever you want in order to encounter your God. If you don't like painting, try eating or maybe just watching a video. Whatever happens, please don't leave." This is like walking into a mall—you don't like Banana Republic? What about Gap? How about an arcade? Or maybe a movie will suit you better? Whatever happens, please don't leave.

In such a setting, people are drawn into personal encounters with God, but they are not woven into the community. They remain individuals who meet God in whatever way is best for them. This is not a center of communal activity. Rather, it is a fragmenting approach to worship that further affirms individualism and undermines the corporate nature of worship.

The problem is not the offering of concurrent options. Instead, the problem arises if people are never invited beyond these options into a corporate practice. Emerging worship may employ a variety of options for encountering God. However, if we want to move beyond private individualism and restore the community of God, at some point in our gatherings we must stop the activities on the margins. We must invite people to the center where we are called to relinquish our own agendas for the sake of participating in worship alongside our brothers and sisters. This corporate act can take many forms, whether it is proclaiming the Word, a responsive reading, or communion. Such corporate, simultaneous practices create (not just reflect) the reality that we are greater than the sum of our parts. We are not a collection of individuals; we are the interconnected body of Christ.

Contemporary worship is often critiqued for being too focused on "me" and not enough on God. Emerging worship has sought to correct this by taking great care to focus our attention on God. However, concurrent elements in worship do little to recover the equally important "us" in worship. A worship service is as much about the gathered community as it is about God. Communion, baptism, confession, and preaching are all acts that depend on the community. By inviting us beyond ourselves into corporate practices, we facilitate the body of Christ and challenge the notion that a relationship with God is first and foremost a private affair.

We also develop a more holistic theology of worship that is personal, corporate, God-focused, and missional. In this sense, worship is not only about God, but it is also about us and our relationships to one another and the world. This is one reason Paul takes great pains to encourage the church in Corinth to be reconciled to one another before they take communion (1 Corinthians 11). In this passage we learn that faithful worship depends upon the health of the community, our practice of justice, and our witness before a watching world.[8]

THE NARRATIVE ARC OF WORSHIP

I remember casually scanning the congregation as I played the guitar in a recent worship service. We had just finished our third song, one extolling the wonders of God and our joy for all God has done. As we started the fourth song with the same spirit of energetic celebration, I caught a glimpse of an unexpected visitor sitting in the back—a good friend of mine who had informed me only a few days earlier that his wife had cheated on him and wanted a divorce. At that moment the lyrics kicked in, and we started singing our joyful thanks for God's abundant blessings. The words I was singing suddenly felt forced, false, and even mocking. I had to spend the rest of the song looking away from my friend, who stood with his mouth shut, staring out the window.

After the worship service I approached him and said, "I was thinking about you the entire service; it must have been painful sitting through the songs we were singing." He responded, "Yeah, it was rough. I'm not sure this is a good time for me to attend church. It is very painful to observe the celebration and not be able to join—it accentuates my loneliness." I remember leaving that worship service thinking there was something very wrong with this situation.

Electronic media culture has a natural bias toward efficiency, entertainment, and consumption. These three values have become the new holy trinity in our culture—to challenge any one of them is an act of heresy. Taking its cues from these biases, worship in the modern church is often equated almost exclusively with joy and celebration. Worship often serves as a kind of pep rally designed to inspire thanksgiving for what God has done and excitement about who God is. While this is certainly a legitimate aspect of worship, it is incomplete.

This comes into full relief when we consider the experience of my friend and even more so when we read through the book of Psalms as a record of ancient worship. This is a book of poetry, liturgy, and hymnody for the people of God and is a rich resource for our worship life today.

Aside from the profound ideas and poetic language, there is an important pattern in the psalms that can serve as a guide to churches seeking to deepen their worship time. The psalms repeatedly employ a narrative arc, a movement from grief and lamentation to celebration and joy. This pattern is strikingly absent from most worship services. We have a strong legacy of denying our suffering in favor of celebration. Perhaps this is because we have the mistaken belief that to acknowledge our suffering might mean we are ungrateful or lacking in faith. More likely it is because grief is an inefficient and unpleasant emotion that stands in direct contradiction to the efficient and entertaining biases of electronic culture. This denial and repression of our heaviest emotions is tragic, and over time it leads to an inauthentic and unhealthy spiritual life.

Authenticity and integrity in worship will mean employing the pattern of the psalms, which express both lament and praise. Each element completes the other. Without lament, praise is little more than shallow sentimentality and a denial of life's struggles and sin. Without praise, lament is a denial of hope and grace, both of which are central to our life of faith and to God's promises.[9] To value one over the other is like suggesting that breathing in is more important than breathing out.

This is not only an issue of authenticity and integrity. It cuts to the heart of hospitality and pastoral sensitivity. For those coming to a worship service immersed in the depth of pain and suffering, celebratory praise takes on a mocking tone that excludes those who are suffering. They are unable to join honestly in these choruses. By incorporating expressions of sorrow, pain, and grief into our worship, the hurting are ushered into God's presence with honesty. At the same time, the rest of the congregation is reminded of the suffering community gathered in their midst. Here they are invited to weep with those who are weeping. By honoring their pain, we acknowledge those who are suffering and affirm them in their grief.

However, worship is not complete without turning to praise and thanksgiving. When pain has been acknowledged, those who suffer are invited beyond their pain to consider God's faithfulness in the midst of suffering and even rejoice with those who are rejoicing. Those who are filled with thanksgiving are allowed the chance to express this before God. These opportunities for lament and praise are not simply about meeting personal needs. They are about the missional practices of authenticity, hospitality, and pastoral care.

This is not simply a technical exhortation for worship planners to use a few songs of lament and a few songs of praise. This is a reminder to consider the powerful ebb and flow of the life of faith, a life punctuated by doubt and hope, despair and healing, repentance and forgiveness. When we plan and develop worship gatherings, this narrative arc should be the backdrop and texture of our worship. The elements included should give space for the variety of profound experiences of our life with God.

The congregation I am part of recently began taking this pattern more seriously. On one occasion we added a step to the communion ritual designed to honor our personal and global grief. On the way up to the front to receive communion, we were served parsley leaves dipped in salt water—a combination that creates a bitter taste. As we ate, the server would say, "Let this taste be a reminder of the world's suffering." The unpleasant taste lingered as we stood in line waiting for the communion elements. The feeling was like a fast; it intensified our longing for the sweet communion elements to rid us of the flavor. When we arrived to partake of the bread and wine, the server would say, "Taste the sweet healing of Christ." It was a ritual that pronounced the power of communion and honored the suffering of those among us.

RECOVERING THE ROLE OF THE ARTIST

For McLuhan, the artist plays a central role in our culture—that of prophet. He writes, "The role of the artist is to create an anti-environment as a means of perception and adjustment. Without an anti-environment all environments are invisible."[10] The artist is the antenna for the future, always probing and finding truths few of us are willing to utter. McLuhan believed the artist would be our best source for revealing the hidden power of our media to shape us. Artists create counterenvironments to help us see the water we swim in, something which is largely invisible to most of us. In one sense it is the role of the artist to focus our gaze on the things we refuse to see or simply cannot see. Like the biblical prophets, artists have often been shunned as unwelcome voices in both the church and broader culture. Fortunately, that tide is turning in the emerging church.

As we continue our journey toward more right brain experiences, a defining mark of the emerging church is a revival of art in worship. This includes art of every kind, not simply painting during a sermon. It is a positive shift in that we are learning once again to welcome the artist as a critical voice in the worshiping community.

Up to this point, this shift has been understood and appreciated for its personal benefits. There is a renewed emphasis on the fact that we are made in the image of God the Creator. As a result, we have revitalized the connection between our Creator and our own creativity. There is growing acceptance that when we create, we participate in the very essence of God's image. In this sense, art moves us into a mysterious communion with our Creator and serves as a kind of spiritual discipline in which art opens unexpected avenues of personal transformation and invites new ways of relating to and experiencing our God. But the greatest gift of this artistic renaissance is not a personal one; rather, it is the gift to the church. As McLuhan observed, it is the gift of the artist as prophet to awaken our souls and sensitize our spirits.

The artist as prophet will inevitably question, challenge, prod, and probe our sensibilities and our assumptions about life, faith, and culture. Artists will open us to new ways of seeing and perceiving. These artists/prophets may use the media of this culture—but often as a way to question it. More often than not art will be inefficient, it will challenge our consumption, and it will entertain only as a by-product, not as its primary objective.

AN ECOLOGY OF WORSHIP

We have covered a lot of ground and perhaps stimulated new questions. How should we use video clips in worship, if at all? If electronic culture communicates with images instead of words, should we do the same with our sermons? Is a preached sermon even relevant anymore? Rather than trying to answer these questions, I believe it is more helpful to offer general guidelines for going forward.

First, we must *probe our media and methods with the right questions*, namely McLuhan's four laws: What does this medium enhance? What will it obsolesce or change the function of? What does it retrieve from the past? What will it reverse into if left unchecked? To these we can add others, such as: What kind of encounter does this medium evoke? In what ways does it limit our experience of God? How does it expand our experience? In what ways could this undermine our intended message? Are we imitating culture? How are we welcoming the artist in our midst? Are we simply providing entertainment? How are we responding to consumer culture? In what ways are we fueling consumerism? These questions stimulate our thinking beyond simple questions of usefulness or effectiveness. They help us to think theologically about our media.

Second, our invitation is to *remember the ecology of the brain*. That may not make sense initially, but consider the brain as a metaphor for our experience in worship. The two opposing hemispheres of the brain might naturally be placed in competing positions; they do not function in that way. Instead, they have achieved an equilibrium or natural ecology in which they are able to function seamlessly together.

Our media forms often have a tendency to stimulate one hemisphere of the brain over the other. You recall that images are processed primarily by the right brain whereas written words are processed more by the left brain. Too often these have needlessly been put in competing positions. Modern worship is characterized by more left brain biases. The emerging church has a tendency to prefer strongly more right brain encounters. However, worship that emphasizes one without the other presents us with a truncated understanding of the gospel and a limited capacity for encountering God. So we are invited to create an ecology of worship that incorporates the experience of both hemispheres.

This goes beyond the word/image debate. Everything from

corporate readings to dance, sculpture, and incense have different biases in the brain. Rather than assuming one medium is categorically better than another, we are better served by considering the ways in which each medium shapes our message and our minds.

SEEING PAST THE SLEIGHT OF HAND

Whether we are using a "Windows" or "Mac" approach to emerging worship, our new forms bring about new ways of thinking, and they have a strong tendency to attract and shape people with postmodern sensibilities. Yet while these new forms shape us in profound ways, they do very little to recover a robust theology of the church or a gospel that points to God's kingdom on earth. It is this, not simply creating new worship forms, that is our most important task. Recovering a theology of the church is not merely a strategy for reaching postmoderns—it is part of our faithfulness to God's work in the world, whether we are in a modern or a postmodern context, whether we are in a print culture or an electronic culture.

The emerging church movement found its origins in its effort to recover a theology of the church as a missional community, not just in the innovation of new worship forms. Unfortunately, the flashy innovations in emerging worship are so attractive that they have occasionally distracted us from the Spirit's deeper and more substantive work in restoring the church. The vitality and survival of what God is doing in the emerging church movement and in electronic culture will depend not upon our ability to elicit experience and participation in worship. Instead it will depend upon our ability to learn together and live out what it means to be the body of Christ, a missional community sent to represent and proclaim the kingdom of God on earth.

EPILOGUE

I was 10 years old when I met William Lo. My dad had returned home from one of his many business trips to China. William was his Chinese counterpart and a translator who had returned with him for a meeting at their corporate headquarters. He became a friend of the family and would stay with us whenever he was in town. He was probably 60 years old, but he didn't look a day over 40.

I remember waking up every morning during his visits and looking out the window to see our Chinese friend in the backyard performing what looked like a slow-motion dance. He would sway and lean as though responding to the wind. His arms would trace controlled arcs in circular movements through the air. I later learned he was a master of an ancient martial art called tai chi and had been performing this two-hour ritual every morning for the last 40 years. My brother and I were enamored with him.

Every now and then William would teach my brother and me a few simple techniques. The one I remember most vividly was how to respond if someone tried to push me. First he modeled the way by inviting us to push him as hard as we could. Eager to play and learn, I backed up and ran straight at him, throwing all my 10-year-old strength into his chest, only to find myself facedown on the ground behind him. It was as though I had traveled right through him.

As I got up, he said, "Now I'm going to push you lightly. Try to resist me with all your strength." I stood my ground as he offered a gentle nudge. The next thing I knew, I was on the ground again. At this point he shared his secret knowledge: "When someone pushes you," he said, "do not resist the force, or it will overtake you. Instead you must understand the force and cooperate with it. Only then will you disarm it." That day William taught us how to relax our upper bodies in such a way as to absorb and deflect the momentum of an outside force. We learned that whatever doesn't bend, breaks. It was a remarkably effective technique that even worked to disarm a schoolyard bully later that year.

William Lo's wise counsel is also appropriate advice as we seek ways to respond to the forces of electronic culture. Instead of simply resisting, critiquing, or caving in to our cultural forces, we are first invited to study and understand them. Only then will we learn to use them rather than being used by them. Only then will we regain our equilibrium and anticipate the powers that shape us.

Like the Maelstrom in Edgar Allan Poe's short story, electronic culture immerses us in an all-at-once, directionless, horizonless, and boundless space. We can neither shut our ears nor avert our gaze, and so we are assailed by unprecedented challenges of forming God's people—the church. In such a world, finding the right answers is of little use. Instead we must recover the ancient art of navigating, perceiving patterns, and learning to probe with different questions.

My great hope is that the conclusions and connections made here are just beginnings for readers. My objective is not to exhaust every possible connection, argument, or answer for how media shapes the church. Instead, my intention is to plant an itch compelling enough for us to scratch. My hope is that we will look at the world and the church in new ways and consider the possibility that things aren't always as they appear.

My prayer is that the ideas contained in this book will help us navigate the challenges of forming God's people in the electronic age with creativity, authenticity, and faithfulness to the gospel.

May God grant us courage, wisdom, and grace as we learn together, try new things, make mistakes, and try again.

BIBLIOGRAPHY

Boorstin, Daniel J. *The Image: A Guide to Pseudo-Events in America.* New York: Vintage, 1987.

Branson, Mark Lau. "Delayed-Disestablishment, the Emerging Church, & All God's People." Last update 2002. *Fuller Theological Seminary. www.fuller.edu/sot/faculty/branson/cp_content/Branson-HomePage.htm.* (Accessed 2004.)

———. "Forming God's People." *Congregations* (Winter 2003). Vol. 29, pp.22-27

Bright, Bill. "The Four Spiritual Laws." Last update 1995. *New Life Publications. www.greatcom. org/laws/english/received.htm.* (Accessed June 28, 2004.)

Burge, Gary M. "Missing God at Church? Why So Many Are Rediscovering Worship in Other Traditions." *Christianity Today* (October 6, 1997): 21-27. Vol.41

Burke, Spencer, and Colleen Pepper. *Making Sense of Church: Eavesdropping on Emerging Conversations About God, Community, and Culture.* Grand Rapids, Mich.: Zondervan, 2003.

Cross, F. L., and Elizabeth A. Livingstone. *The Oxford Dictionary of the Christian Church*, 3rd ed. New York: Oxford University Press, 1997.

Crouch, Andy. "A Community of Foes." *Re:generation Quarterly* (Winter 2001). Vol.7, p.3

Edinger, Edward F. *The Eternal Drama: The Inner Meaning of Greek Mythology*, 1st ed. Boston: Shambhala, Random House, 1994.

Freire, Paulo. *Pedagogy of the Oppressed*, new rev. 20th-anniversary ed. New York: Continuum, 1993.

Gibbs, Eddie. *Churchnext: Quantum Changes in How We Do Ministry.* Downers Grove, Ill.: Inter-Varsity Press, 2000.

———. "Signs of an Emerging Church." *Fuller Focus* (Spring 2004). Vol. 12, pp.4-6.

Gordon, W. Terrence. *Marshall McLuhan: Escape into Understanding: A Biography.* Toronto: Stoddart, 1997.

———. *McLuhan for Beginners.* New York: Writers and Readers, 1997.

Gozzi, Raymond Jr. "Paradoxes of Electric Media." *EME: Explorations in Media Ecology* 3, no. 2 (2004): 127-30.

Grenz, Stanley J. *A Primer on Postmodernism.* Grand Rapids, Mich.: William B. Eerdmans, 1996.

———. *Theology for the Community of God.* Grand Rapids, Mich.: William B. Eerdmans, 2000.

Guder, Darrell L., and Lois Barrett. *Missional Church: A Vision for the Sending of the Church in North America (The Gospel and Our Culture Series).* Grand Rapids, Mich.: William B. Eerdmans, 1998.

Janz, Denis. *A Reformation Reader: Primary Texts with Introductions.* Minneapolis: Fortress, 1999.

Jefferson, David J. "The Pop Prophets." *Newsweek* (May 24, 2004): 44-50. Vol. 143

Jones, Tony. *Soul Shaper: Exploring Spirituality and Contemplative Practices in Youth Ministry.* Grand Rapids, Mich.: Youth Specialties, 2003.

Kimball, Dan. *The Emerging Church: Vintage Christianity for New Generations.* Grand Rapids, Mich.: Zondervan, 2003.

————. *Emerging Worship: Creating Worship Gatherings for New Generations.* Grand Rapids, Mich.: emergentYS/Zondervan, 2004.

Latourette, Kenneth Scott. *The Chinese, Their History and Culture,* 4th ed. New York: Macmillan, 1964.

Lazin, Dan. "Better Living: Too Many Social Experiments Start with the Best Intentions and End in Disaster." *This Magazine* (June 2003). Vol. 36, pp.32-35

Lohfink, Gerhard. *Jesus and Community: The Social Dimension of Christian Faith.* Philadelphia: Fortress, 1984.

London, H. B., Jr., and Neil B. Wiseman. *Pastors at Greater Risk,* rev. ed. Ventura, Calif.: Gospel Light, 2003.

Lyotard, Jean François. *The Postmodern Condition: A Report on Knowledge.* Trans. by Geoff Bennington and Brian Massumi. Minneapolis: University of Minnesota Press, 1984.

McLuhan, Marshall. *The Mechanical Bride: Folklore of Industrial Man.* Corte Madera, Calif.: Gingko, 2002.

————. *Understanding Media: The Extensions of Man,* 1st MIT Press ed. Cambridge, Mass.: MIT Press, 1994.

McLuhan, Marshall, David Carson, and Eric McLuhan. *The Book of Probes,* 1st ed. Corte Madera, Calif.: Gingko, 2003.

McLuhan, Marshall, and Quentin Fiore. *The Medium Is the Message: An Inventory of Effects.* San Francisco: HardWired, 1996.

McLuhan, Marshall, and Eric McLuhan. *Laws of Media: The New Science.* Toronto: University of Toronto Press, 1988.

McLuhan, Marshall, Eric McLuhan, and Jacek Szlarek. *The Medium and the Light: Reflections on Religion.* Toronto; New York: Stoddart, 1999.

McLuhan, Marshall, Eric McLuhan, and Frank Zingrone. *Essential McLuhan,* 1st ed. New York: BasicBooks, 1995.

Meyrowitz, Joshua. *No Sense of Place: The Impact of Electronic Media on Social Behavior.* New York: Oxford University Press, 1985.

Miller, M. Rex. *The Millennium Matrix: Reclaiming the Past, Reframing the Future of the Church.* San Francisco: Jossey-Bass, 2004.

Murphy, Nancey. *Anglo-American Postmodernity: Philosophical Perspective on Science, Religion, and Ethics.* Boulder, Colo.: Westview, 1997.

Ong, Walter J. *Orality and Literacy: The Technologizing of the Word.* London; New York: Methuen, 1982.

Phillips, Stone, "Behind the Apprentice: Dateline with Stone Phillips," Directed by Marsha Bartel. *Airdate* April 14, 2004. Television.

Plato, and Walter Hamilton. *Phaedrus, and, the Seventh and Eighth Letters.* Harmondsworth, U.K.: Penguin, 1973.

Poe, Edgar Allan. "A Descent into the Maelstrom." In *The Complete Tales and Poems of Edgar Allan Poe.* New York: The Modern Library, 1935.

Postman, Neil. *Amusing Ourselves to Death: Public Discourse in the Age of Show Business.* New York: Penguin, 1986.

———. *The Disappearance of Childhood,* 1st Vintage ed. New York: Vintage, 1994.

———. *Technopoly: The Surrender of Culture to Technology,* 1st Vintage ed. New York: Vintage, 1993.

Quine, Willard V., and J. S. Ullian. *The Web of Belief.* New York: Random House, 1970.

Roxburgh, Alan J. *The Missionary Congregation, Leadership & Liminality, Christian Mission and Modern Culture.* Harrisburg, Pa.: Trinity Press International, 1997.

Sample, Tex. *The Spectacle of Worship in a Wired World: Electronic Culture and the Gathered People of God.* Nashville, Tenn.: Abingdon, 1998.

Schultze, Quentin J. *Habits of the High-Tech Heart: Living Virtuously in the Information Age.* Grand Rapids, Mich.: Baker, 2002.

Smith, Sarah. "E-Mail Etiquette." *Psychology Today* (July/August 2000) Vol.33, p.14

Sobelman, David, *McLuhan's Wake.* Directed by Kevin McMahon. Primitive Entertainment and The National Film Board of Canada; Montreal, 2002. VHS tape.

Sweet, Leonard I., and Andy Crouch et al. *The Church in Emerging Culture: Five Perspectives.* El Cajon, Calif.: emergentYS/Zondervan, 2003.

Tarnas, Richard. *The Passion of the Western Mind: Understanding the Ideas That Have Shaped Our World View,* 1st ed. New York: Harmony, 1991.

Van Gelder, Craig. *Confident Witness—Changing World: Rediscovering the Gospel in North America, The Gospel and Our Culture Series.* Grand Rapids, Mich.: William B. Eerdmans, 1999.

Volf, Miroslav. *After Our Likeness: The Church as the Image of the Trinity (Sacra Doctrina).* Grand Rapids, Mich.: William B. Eerdmans, 1998.

Warren, Rick. "Evangelizing the 21st Century Culture." Last updated January 7, 2004. *pastors.com. www.pastors.com/RWMT/default.asp?id=136&artid=4545&expand=1* (Accessed April 19, 2004.)

Whitefield, George. *Selected Sermons of George Whitefield.* Oak Harbor, Wash.: Logos Research Systems, 1999.

Witvliet, John D. *Worship Seeking Understanding: Windows into Christian Practice.* Grand Rapids, Mich.: Baker Academic, 2003.

Wolf, Gary. "Channeling McLuhan." *Wired* (January 1996). Vol.4, pp.128-131

Yoder, John Howard. *Body Politics: Five Practices of the Christian Community Before the Watching World.* Scottsdale, Pa.: Herald, 1992.

ENDNOTES

Introduction

[1] Eddie Gibbs, "Signs of an Emerging Church," *Fuller Focus* (Spring 2004): 4. Vol.12

[2] Darrell L. Guder and Lois Barrett, *Missional Church: A Vision for the Sending of the Church in North America (The Gospel and Our Culture Series)* (Grand Rapids, Mich.: William B. Eerdmans, 1998), 79-85.

Chapter One: Seeing but not Perceiving

[1] Marshall McLuhan, Eric McLuhan, and Jacek Szlarek, *The Medium and the Light: Reflections on Religion* (Toronto; New York: Stoddart, 1999), 117.

[2] Plato and Walter Hamilton, *Phaedrus and the Seventh and Eighth Letters* (Harmondsworth, England: Penguin, 1973), 96.

[3] Quentin J. Schultze, *Habits of the High-Tech Heart: Living Virtuously in the Information Age* (Grand Rapids, Mich.: Baker, 2002), 21.

[4] Neil Postman, *Technopoly: The Surrender of Culture to Technology, 1st Vintage ed.* (New York: Vintage, 1993), 5.

[5] Ibid.

Chapter Two: Perceiving the Powers That Shape Us

[1] Rick Warren, *Evangelizing the 21st Century Culture.* Cited January 7, 2004. *pastors.com: www.pastors.com/RWMT/default.asp?id=136&artid=4545&expand=1* (Accessed April 19, 2004).

[2] Marshall McLuhan, *Understanding Media: The Extensions of Man,* 1st MIT Press ed. (Cambridge, Mass.: MIT Press, 1994), 7.

[3] W. Terrence Gordon, *Marshall McLuhan: Escape into Understanding: A Biography* (Toronto: Stoddart, 1997), 226.

[4] W. Terrence Gordon, *McLuhan for Beginners* (New York: Writers and Readers, 1997), 2.

[5] Cited in Marshall McLuhan, Eric McLuhan, and Frank Zingrone, *Essential McLuhan,* 1st ed. (New York: BasicBooks, 1995), 233.

[6] McLuhan, *Understanding Media: The Extensions of Man,* x.

[7] Ibid.

[8] Marshall McLuhan and Eric McLuhan, *Laws of Media: The New Science* (Toronto: University of Toronto Press, 1988), 239.

[9] Gary Wolf, "Channeling McLuhan," *Wired* (January 1996): Vol.4, p.128

[10] A collection of articles, essays, and letters on McLuhan's media theory of the church was published posthumously in McLuhan, McLuhan, and Szlarek, *The Medium and the Light: Reflections on Religion.*

[11] Ibid., 85.

[12] Marshall McLuhan, *The Mechanical Bride: Folklore of Industrial Man* (Corte Madera, Calif.: Gingko, 2002), v.

[13] David Sobelman, *McLuhan's Wake,* Directed by Kevin McMahon. Primitive Entertainment and The National Film Board of Canada; Montreal, 2002. VHS tape.

[14] Edgar Allan Poe, "A Descent into the Maelstrom," in *The Complete Tales and Poems of Edgar Allan Poe* (New York: The Modern Library, 1935), 135.

[15] McLuhan, *Understanding Media: The Extensions of Man,* 41ff.

[16] Edward F. Edinger, *The Eternal Drama: The Inner Meaning of Greek Mythology,* 1st ed. (Boston: Shambhala, Random House, 1994), 85f.

[17] Warren, *Evangelizing the 21st Century Culture,* Cited.

[18] McLuhan, *Understanding Media: The Extensions of Man,* 18.

[19] McLuhan, McLuhan, and Zingrone, *Essential McLuhan,* 238.

[20] To understand why this is important, it is helpful to consider what graphic designers and visual artists call the *figure/ground* relationship. This refers to the way we perceive things in pictures. Think of a painting that depicts a ball in an empty room. The ball in the painting is considered the "figure" or main object of the painting, whereas the empty room is the "ground" or backdrop. Most of the time we are focused on the figure and ignore the ground. But painters and designers recognize that the ground is equally, if not more, important than the figure to the beauty of the painting.

In the same way, if we consider the TV medium as the *ground* and the TV message as the *figure,* too often we focus only on the *figure* and ignore the *ground.* Instead, we must learn to perceive the interplay of these two things (figure/ground) to truly perceive the power and effects of media.

To understand how this interplay between *figure* and *ground* is important, consider the image below. This is a well-known photograph of melting snow.

As the story goes, it was taken by a Chinese man who had a recent encounter with Christian missionaries. For several days he was distraught by what he learned from them and was filled with questions about the truth of Jesus. One day, as he was hiking up in the hills, he came upon this patch of melting snow where large blotches of dark earth were peeking through. He gazed at it for a moment until he was startled to find he was looking at the face of Christ. In his excitement he took this photograph; and taking it as a sign, he became a Christian on the spot.

It is not uncommon for those who see this image for the first time to see only a random assortment of abstract shapes. This is because many of us initially mistake the black shapes as the foreground (i.e., *figure*) and the white shapes as the background (i.e., *ground*). But when one considers the white shapes to be the foreground and the black shapes as the background, the image of Jesus comes into full relief. In the same way when we view our media and methods through this lens, we will see things very differently. This is crucial for helping us detect the hidden effects of our media. McLuhan used this illustration in an interview published in *McLuhan, McLuhan, and Szlarek,* The Medium and the Light: Reflections on Religion, 103.

[21] Gordon, *Marshall McLuhan: Escape into Understanding: A Biography,* 309.

[22] McLuhan and McLuhan, *Laws of Media: The New Science,* 93.

[23] Ibid., 239.

Chapter Three: Printing: the Architect of the Modern Church

[1] Marshall McLuhan and Quentin Fiore, *The Medium Is the Message: An Inventory of Effects* (San Francisco, Calif.: HardWired, 1996), 50.

[2] McLuhan, *Understanding Media: The Extensions of Man*, xxi.

[3] Ibid, quoted, 81.

[4] Walter J. Ong, *Orality and Literacy: The Technologizing of the Word* (London; New York: Methuen, 1982), 82.

[5] Kenneth Scott Latourette, *The Chinese, Their History and Culture*, 4th ed. (New York: Macmillan, 1964), 310.

[6] Ong, *Orality and Literacy: The Technologizing of the Word*, 87.

[7] McLuhan, *Understanding Media: The Extensions of Man*, 83.

[8] Ong, *Orality and Literacy: The Technologizing of the Word*, 24.

[9] Postman, *Technopoly: The Surrender of Culture to Technology*, 65.

[10] Richard Tarnas, *The Passion of the Western Mind: Understanding the Ideas That Have Shaped Our World View*, 1st ed. (New York: Harmony, 1991), 225f.

[11] McLuhan, *Understanding Media: The Extensions of Man*, 171.

[12] McLuhan, McLuhan, and Zingrone, *Essential McLuhan*, 244.

[13] Ong, *Orality and Literacy: The Technologizing of the Word*, 78.

[14] Gerhard Lohfink, *Jesus and Community: The Social Dimension of Christian Faith* (Philadelphia: Fortress, 1984), 3.

[15] Ong, *Orality and Literacy: The Technologizing of the Word*, 24.

[16] This calculation is based on the word count of Edwards' sermons, several of which were over 18,000 words long. A 30-minute sermon is typically only 2,000 words long.

[17] George Whitefield, *Selected Sermons of George Whitefield* (Oak Harbor, Wash.: Logos Research Systems, 1999).

[18] F. L. Cross and Elizabeth A. Livingstone, *The Oxford Dictionary of the Christian Church*, 3rd ed. (Oxford; New York: Oxford University Press, 1997), 532.

[19] Ibid., 702.

[20] Bill Bright, "The Four Spiritual Laws" [New Life Publications, 1995]. Cited June 28, 2004. *www.greatcom. org/laws/english/received.htm* (Accessed June 28, 2004).

Chapter Four: Electronic Media: Planting the Seeds of the Emerging Church

[1] McLuhan, McLuhan, and Zingrone, *Essential McLuhan*, 245.

[2] Marshall McLuhan, David Carson, and Eric McLuhan, *The Book of Probes*, 1st ed. (Corte Madera, Calif.: Gingko, 2003), 109.

[3] Neil Postman, *The Disappearance of Childhood*, 1st Vintage ed. (New York: Vintage, 1994), 68.

[4] Stanley J. Grenz, *A Primer on Postmodernism* (Grand Rapids, Mich.: William B. Eerdmans, 1996), 83.

[5] McLuhan, *Understanding Media: The Extensions of Man*, xxi.

[6] Some recent literature has focused on key differences between "electronic" media and "digital" media. See Craig Van Gelder, *Confident Witness—Changing World: Rediscovering the Gospel in North America, (The Gospel and Our Culture Series)* (Grand Rapids, Mich.: William B. Eerdmans, 1999), 26f. Rex Miller also makes a distinction between "broadcast culture" and "digital culture." See M. Rex Miller, *The Millennium Matrix: Reclaiming the Past, Reframing the Future of the Church* (San Francisco: Jossey-Bass, 2004). 76ff

While I am aware of these debates, I do not find them useful for this discussion. As a result, I will use the terms "electronic" and "digital" interchangeably.

[7] Leonard I. Sweet and Andy Crouch, et al., *The Church in Emerging Culture: Five Perspectives* (El Cajon, Calif.: emergentYS/Zondervan, 2003) 32f.

[8] Postman, *The Disappearance of Childhood*, 72.

[9] Daniel J. Boorstin, *The Image: A Guide to Pseudo-Events in America* (New York: Vintage, 1987), 13.

[10] Postman, *Technopoly: The Surrender of Culture to Technology*, 67.

[11] Neil Postman, *Amusing Ourselves to Death: Public Discourse in the Age of Show Business* (New York: Penguin, 1986), 69.

[12] Postman, *The Disappearance of Childhood*, 106.

[13] Jean François Lyotard, *The Postmodern Condition: A Report on Knowledge,* trans. Geoff Bennington and Brian Massumi (Minneapolis: University of Minnesota Press, 1994), iv.

[14] See chapters 5 and 6 in Nancey Murphy, *Anglo-American Postmodernity: Philosophical Perspective on Science, Religion, and Ethics* (Boulder, Colo.: Westview Press, 1997).

[15] Willard V. Quine and J. S. Ullian, *The Web of Belief* (New York,: Random House, 1970).

[16] McLuhan, *Understanding Media: The Extensions of Man*, 300.

[17] Ibid., 84.

[18] Postman, *The Disappearance of Childhood*, 73.

[19] Ibid.

[20] McLuhan and McLuhan, *Laws of Media: The New Science,* 67f.

[21] Gary M. Burge, "Missing God at Church? Why So Many Are Rediscovering Worship in Other Traditions," *Christianity Today* (October 6, 1997). pp. 21-23

[22] Tony Jones, *Soul Shaper: Exploring Spirituality and Contemplative Practices in Youth Ministry* (Grand Rapids, Mich.: Youth Specialties, 2003), 108.

[23] Dan Kimball, *Emerging Worship: Creating Worship Gatherings for New Generations* (Grand Rapids, Mich.: emergentYS/Zondervan, 2004) 81f.

[24] Denis R. Janz, ed., et al., *A Reformation Reader: Primary Texts with Introductions* (Minneapolis: Fortress, 1999), 109.

[25] This shift is noted in Spencer Burke and Colleen Pepper, *Making Sense of Church: Eavesdropping on Emerging Conversations About God, Community, and Culture* (Grand Rapids, Mich.: Zondervan, 2003), 143-159.

[26] Postman, *Amusing Ourselves to Death: Public Discourse in the Age of Show Business,* 72.

Chapter Five: Evolving the Medium and the Message

[1] McLuhan, *Understanding Media: The Extensions of Man*, 48.

[2] McLuhan and Fiore, *The Medium Is the Message: An Inventory of Effects,* 25.

[3] Ibid.

[4] McLuhan, McLuhan, and Szlarek, *The Medium and the Light: Reflections on Religion,* 103.

[5] Lohfink, *Jesus and Community: The Social Dimension of Christian Faith,* 122.

[6] Guder and Barrett, *Missional Church: A Vision for the Sending of the Church in North America,* 101.

[7] Mark Lau Branson, *Delayed-Disestablishment, the Emerging Church, & All God's People.* Last updated 2002. Fuller Theological Seminary: *www.fuller.edu/sot/faculty/branson/cp_content/BransonHomePage.htm.* (Accessed 2004).

Chapter Six: Community in Electronic Culture

[1] McLuhan, *Understanding Media: The Extensions of Man*, 50f.

[2] McLuhan and Fiore, *The Medium Is the Message: An Inventory of Effects*, 67.

[3] Raymond Jr. Gozzi, "Paradoxes of Electric Media," *EME: Explorations in Media Ecology*, 3, no. 2 (2004): 127.

[4] Joshua Meyrowitz, *No Sense of Place: The Impact of Electronic Media on Social Behavior* (New York: Oxford University Press, 1985), 133.

[5] Stone Philips, "Behind The Apprentice," *Dateline with Stone Phillips*, directed by Marsha Bartel. Airdate April 14, 2004. Television show episode.

[6] Stanley J. Grenz, *Theology for the Community of God* (Grand Rapids, Mich.: William B. Eerdmans, 2000), xxxi.

[7] Miroslav Volf, *After Our Likeness: The Church as the Image of the Trinity* (Sacra Doctrina) (Grand Rapids, Mich.: William B. Eerdmans, 1998), x.

[8] Dan Lazin, "Better Living: Too Many Social Experiments Start with the Best Intentions and End in Disaster," *This Magazine* (June 2003). pp.32-35

[9] David J. Jefferson, "The Pop Prophets," Newsweek (May 24, 2004): 46.

[10] Postman, *Technopoly: The Surrender of Culture to Technology*, 66.

[11] This phrase is taken from the title of Meyrowitz, *No Sense of Place: The Impact of Electronic Media on Social Behavior*.

[12] Gozzi, "Paradoxes of Electric Media": 128

[13] Mark Lau Branson, "Forming God's People," *Congregations* (Winter 2003) Vol.29, pp. 22-27

[14] Sarah Smith, "E-Mail Etiquette," *Psychology Today* (July/August 2000): 4. Vol. 33

[15] Andy Crouch, "A Community of Foes," *Re:generation Quarterly* (Winter 2001): 3. Vol. 7

[16] John Howard Yoder, *Body Politics: Five Practices of the Christian Community Before the Watching World* (Scottsdale, Pa.: Herald, 1992), 13.

Chapter Seven: Leadership in Electronic Culture

[1] McLuhan, McLuhan, and Szlarek, *The Medium and the Light: Reflections on Religion*, 85.

[2] Ibid., 56.

[3] Burke and Pepper, *Making Sense of Church: Eavesdropping on Emerging Conversations About God, Community, and Culture*, 36. See also Eddie Gibbs, *Churchnext: Quantum Changes in How We Do Ministry* (Downers Grove, Ill.: InterVarsity Press, 2000), 35ff.

[4] Meyrowitz, *No Sense of Place: The Impact of Electronic Media on Social Behavior*, 64.

[5] Postman, *The Disappearance of Childhood*, 79. Postman is quoting from a chapter of an unpublished work by Reginald Damerall of the University of Massachusetts.

[6] Remarkably, many book publishers are increasingly attempting to mirror this blogging pattern in books by adding multiple author commentaries in margins and rejoinders. While such an effort is an understandable response to a threatening new medium, it seems to me these publishers misunderstand the power of their medium. The form of a book is ill-suited to dynamic dialogue in the same way that blogs are ill-suited to express extensive, precise, and thorough analysis. To attempt either is like using a 747 to deliver mail between L.A. and San Diego. It is possible to do, but it grossly underutilizes the medium.

[7] I worked for a company that specialized in Internet usability testing; this was one of the most common findings we discovered.

[8] This discussion of praxis is expressed more fully in Paulo Freire, *Pedagogy of the Oppressed*, new rev. 20th-anniversary ed. (New York: Continuum, 1993). Mark Lau Branson used the specific language of "study/reflection" and "action/engagement" to make Freire's ideas more accessible.

[9] Branson, "Forming God's People." Vol.29, pp. 22-27

[10] Adapted from a Pasadena Mennonite Church document.

Chapter Eight: Worship in Electronic Culture

[1] McLuhan, *Understanding Media: The Extensions of Man*, 321.

[2] Dan Kimball, *The Emerging Church: Vintage Christianity for New Generations* (Grand Rapids, Mich.: Zondervan, 2003), 7. See also Kimball, *Emerging Worship: Creating Worship Gatherings for New Generations*, 17.

[3] Tex Sample, *The Spectacle of Worship in a Wired World: Electronic Culture and the Gathered People of God* (Nashville, Tenn.: Abingdon, 1998). 92.

[4] McLuhan, McLuhan, and Szlarek, *The Medium and the Light: Reflections on Religion*, 204.

[5] McLuhan and Fiore, *The Medium Is the Message: An Inventory of Effects*, 48.

[6] Alan J. Roxburgh, *The Missionary Congregation, Leadership & Liminality*, Christian Mission and Modern Culture (Harrisburg, Pa.: Trinity Press International, 1997), 12.

[7] H. B. London, Jr. and Neil B. Wiseman, *Pastors at Greater Risk*, rev. ed. (Ventura, Calif.: Gospel Light, 2003). p. 33ff

[8] Yoder, *Body Politics: Five Practices of the Christian Community Before the Watching World*, 18.

[9] John D. Witvliet, *Worship Seeking Understanding: Windows into Christian Practice* (Grand Rapids, Mich.: Baker Academic, 2003), 40.

[10] McLuhan, Carson, and McLuhan, *The Book of Probes*, 30.